# BREEDING BIOLOGY OF THE EGYPTIAN PLOVER,
Pluvianus aegyptius

Pair of *Pluvianus aegyptius* with two newly hatched chicks (from eggs 4a-b, table 1).

BREEDING BIOLOGY OF THE EGYPTIAN PLOVER, *Pluvianus aegyptius*

BY
THOMAS R. HOWELL

UNIVERSITY OF CALIFORNIA PUBLICATIONS IN ZOOLOGY
Volume 113

UNIVERSITY OF CALIFORNIA PRESS

591.08
C153u
v.113
1979

BREEDING BIOLOGY OF THE EGYPTIAN PLOVER,
Pluvianus aegyptius

BY
THOMAS R. HOWELL

UNIVERSITY OF CALIFORNIA PRESS
BERKELEY • LOS ANGELES • LONDON
1979

UNIVERSITY OF CALIFORNIA PUBLICATIONS IN ZOOLOGY

Volume 113

Approved for publication: July 28, 1978

UNIVERSITY OF CALIFORNIA PRESS
BERKELEY AND LOS ANGELES
CALIFORNIA

UNIVERSITY OF CALIFORNIA PRESS, LTD.
LONDON, ENGLAND

ISBN 0-520-03804-5
LIBRARY OF CONGRESS CATALOG CARD NUMBER 78-64476
COPYRIGHT © 1979 BY THE REGENTS OF THE UNIVERSITY OF CALIFORNIA

PRINTED IN THE UNITED STATES OF AMERICA

CONTENTS

Abstract	1
Introduction	2
Acknowledgments	2
Historical Review	3
The Study Area and Local Conditions	7
General Natural History	8
Activities Independent of Breeding	8
Feeding Behavior of Adults	8
Body Maintenance and Comfort Activities	10
Activities Related to Breeding	12
Attainment of Breeding Condition	12
Tameness	12
Vocalizations	13
Individual Recognition	14
Nesting Sites	16
Territoriality	16
Size of the Territory	18
Alert and Aggressive Displays	18
Nesting Behavior	21
Scrape-making	21
Copulation	25
Eggs	26
Incubation Behavior	26
Soaking	31
Incubation Period	33
Second Clutches	35
Pipping	36
Hatching	36
Roles of the Parents During Hatching	37
Activity of Newly-hatched Chicks	37
Covering of Young Birds with Sand	40
Incubation Temperatures	42
Physiology of Incubation	51
Introductory Review	51
Adult Body Weight, Egg Weight, and Incubation Period	54
Egg Weight Loss, Conductance, and Water Vapor Pressure in the Nest	56
Shell Thickness and Weight	63
Chick Weight	65
Fledging Period	65
Discussion	65
Egg-burying	66
Soaking and Nest-wetting	67

Chick-burying 67
　　　Adult Plumage Pattern 68
　　　Incubation Period and Fledging Period 69
　　　Phylogeny 72
References 75
Plates 77

BREEDING BIOLOGY OF THE EGYPTIAN PLOVER, *PLUVIANUS AEGYPTIUS* (AVES: GLAREOLIDAE)

BY

THOMAS R. HOWELL

ABSTRACT

The Egyptian Plover breeds only in tropical Africa along rivers where sandbars are exposed by low water during the dry season. This species is noted for two unusual behavior patterns attributed to it: (1) picking food particles from the jaws and teeth of basking crocodiles; and (2) burying its eggs in the sand and leaving them to be incubated by solar heat. Pattern (1), accounts of which date back to Herodotus, is not incontrovertibly documented and I never observed it. Pattern (2) is more complex than is stated and was a principal subject of my study.

I studied a population of this species (abbreviated as EP) at Gambela, along the Baro River, Ilubabor Province, southwestern Ethiopia, from 24 January to 6 April 1977. The birds are strikingly patterned and the sexes are indistinguishable in color, vocalizations, and size; adults weigh about 78 g during the nesting period. Most birds were paired and territorial at the time of my arrival. Both sexes defend a territory on a sandbar island by threat displays and fighting. They attempt to drive off all other EPs and all potential competitors and predators. Courtship activity and precopulatory displays are simple and minimal. The nest is a scrape in the sand-gravel substrate, and both sexes make many preliminary scrapes before one is finally chosen. The usual clutch at Gambela is two or three eggs (one single-egg clutch); the mean egg weight is 9.5 g. From the first, eggs are covered with sand (by use of the bill, not the feet) to a usual depth of 2 mm to 3 mm above their upper surface. The parents in turn sit on the nest most of the day and may sometimes bring the egg surface in contact with the incubation patch by scraping away sand with the feet while sitting. Whenever an adult leaves the nest it quickly throws sand over the site with the bill. At night the eggs are about two-thirds uncovered and continuously incubated. During the six hottest hours of the day, each adult frequently soaks its ventral feathers in the river and returns to settle on the buried eggs, thus keeping them surrounded by wet sand. The soaking is a stereotyped activity and is done only after the first egg is laid and when ambient temperatures are high.

The incubation period is about 30 days, and chicks hatch from eggs under the sand. Chicks are highly precocial and leave the nest permanently by the end of the day of hatching. The parents bring some food to the chicks and also expose food for them by stone-turning and other foraging methods. At any approach of danger, chicks crouch down and are completely covered with sand by a parent in the same manner that eggs are covered. Buried chicks are also wetted with soaked ventral feathers. Chicks remain immobile if excavated and gently handled but will suddenly flee if extensively manipulated. Even juveniles up to three weeks of age may be covered with sand by a parent. By the age of about four weeks, juveniles have acquired contour feathers with the adult color pattern, and I estimate the age of first flight as about 35 days.

I measured the incubation temperature (T_E) using a fresh egg implanted with a thermocouple as a replacement for one of a pair's own eggs, and simultaneously recorded relevant ambient temperatures. On a typical day, the parents attend the buried eggs only occasionally during the first three hours after sunrise (0700). A balanced combination of body heat, solar heat, and heat retained by the sand keeps T_E within appropriate limits. The birds often poke the bill in the sand around the eggs, possibly testing the temperature. By about 1000 to 1030, air temperature in the shade approaches 40° and continues rising to peaks of 45° to 46° (over 50° in sun). For about the next six hours the adults cool the eggs by wetting them every few minutes with soaked ventral feathers (river temperature 27°). As shaded air temperatures and subsurface dry sand temperatures often exceed 45°, mere shading of the buried eggs would not prevent overheating. By about 1600 solar heat begins to decline and the birds become less attentive and cease soaking. T_E sometimes briefly reaches 42°, but all undamaged, nonimplanted eggs in monitored nests hatched. I estimated mean incubation temperature over twenty-four hours as 37.5°.

I measured daily weight loss ($\dot{M}_{H_2O}$) of eggs due to water vapor loss, in natural nests and in a silica gel desiccator, and calculated the fraction (F) of initial egg weight lost and eggshell conductance (G_{H_2O} = water loss·day^{-1}·torr^{-1}); the latter is a measure of the porosity of the shell. I also placed silica gel-filled eggshells in nests and measured weight gain (= water uptake). I compared these figures with those predicted on the basis of initial egg weight and incubation period (which is much longer than predicted from initial weight). $\dot{M}_{H_2O}$ and F are significantly lower than predicted, but G_{H_2O} is not. This indicates that the low figures for $\dot{M}_{H_2O}$ and F are not the result of modifications in the porosity of the shell. I hypothesize that the soaking of the eggs for about six hours each day greatly reduces daily water loss from the egg and permits a long incubation period without excessive dehydration. I further hypothesize that the long incubation period is adaptively advantageous by allowing enough time for prehatching maturation to produce a highly precocial chick, necessary for survival on an open sandbar island. I propose that concealment was the initial adaptive advantage to egg-burying, and that the combination of burying and wetting enables the EP to nest in a habitat where the eggs would otherwise be lethally overheated.

The EP's conspicuous pattern makes concealment of the incubating adults impossible, but covering-wetting of the eggs makes it possible for the adults to leave the nest safely while distracting or attacking approaching predators or competitors. The display of striking plumage patterns is often effective in repelling adversaries without a fight. The success of *Pluvianus aegyptius*—the only species of courser to colonize the fluviatile habitat—is attributable to its methods of incubation and chick care, which are unique among birds.

INTRODUCTION

The Egyptian Plover (*Pluvianus aegyptius*) lives along rivers throughout the lowlands of tropical Africa except in the heavily forested regions and most of the area east of the Rift Valley (Mackworth-Praed and Grant, 1952, 1970). The species formerly occurred north of the tropics all along the Nile, but great ecological changes in that region since the nineteenth century have resulted in its disappearance from the northernmost part of its previous range. In historic times the breeding range has been entirely within Africa and only stray individuals have been recorded outside that continent. The Egyptian Plover breeds only along those rivers where open areas of sand and gravel are exposed by low water levels during the dry season and provide the type of substrate in which it nests. It does not regularly occur around lakes and is generally absent from coastal areas except where rivers reach the sea.

The species was described by Linnaeus in 1758 as *Charadrius aegyptius* from specimens collected in Egypt where it was once abundant, hence the vernacular name Egyptian Plover. This is now a double misnomer as the bird is no longer known to occur in Egypt and as it is not a true plover (Charadriidae) but a courser (Cursoriinae, Glareolidae). For these reasons I will abbreviate the inappropriate vernacular name to EP and use this except when it might cause confusion or when more formal nomenclature is desirable.

The EP is a strikingly marked bird and no other species closely resembles it (frontispiece). The sexes are identical in size and external appearance. Spreading of the wings reveals an unusual and sharply contrasting white and black pattern that is importantly used in displays (pls. 1, 2). The following color details are not always evident in museum specimens or their accompanying data: the iris is dark and does not contrast with the surrounding black feathers; the bill in adults is entirely black, inside and out; the legs and feet are blue-gray. Adults are about 22 cm long and weigh between about 75 to 90 g, depending on the season (p. 54).

Acknowledgments

I gratefully acknowledge the support, advice, and assistance of the organizations and individuals that made it possible for me to conduct this study. The National Geographic Society provided financial support through a grant from its Committee on Research and Exploration. I received useful information by correspondence from many people, including J. C. Farrand, C. H. Fry, C. T. Collins, and G. L. Maclean. Permission to carry out the research in Gambela was obtained through the cooperation of the Wildlife Conservation Organization of the Provisional Military Socialist Government of Ethiopia, Ato Teshoma Ashine, General Manager, and Mr. J. G. Stephenson, Senior Advisor. Mr. and Mrs. Stephenson were helpful and hospitable in many other ways. The personnel of U. S. Naval Medical Research Unit No. 5 (NAMRU-5), Addis Ababa, aided me in innumerable ways and especially in the shipment of equipment. In Gambela, Dr. and Mrs. D. Reynolds and the Rev. R. McLaughlin kindly offered medical advice and information about local conditions, and Charles Fields of the United Nations Food and Agriculture Organization provided help and companionship when it was most needed. The people of Gambela, in all walks of life, were friendly to me and tolerant of my activities. I am particularly grateful to Dr. John S. Ash (formerly Head, Medical Ecology Division, NAMRU-5) and Jonquil Ash for their generous and wholehearted cooperation, encouragement, and aid in every possible way; without their unfailing assistance, the field work could not have been accomplished.

The Western Foundation of Vertebrate Zoology, Los Angeles, California kindly provided the use of their oölogical study facilities and the expert services of R. Quigley, Jr., who made black and white prints for the plates from my color transparencies. I also thank J. L. Hand and C. H. Jacobs for making the sound spectrograms and for discussions concerning them.

I have benefited greatly from critical comments of the following people who have read all or part of the manuscript: G. A. Bartholomew, H. Rahn, D. F. Hoyt, C. M. and D. Vleck. Their helpful interest does not necessarily imply endorsement of my interpretations, for which I am fully responsible.

HISTORICAL REVIEW

The EP is well-known to ornithologists because of two unusual patterns of behavior attributed to it: (1) it is alleged to pick food from the jaws and teeth of basking crocodiles (*Crocodilus niloticus*); and (2) it buries its eggs in the sand and has been alleged to leave them for most of the day, either to be incubated by or protected from solar heat, or some combination thereof. I will consider the first of these allegations only briefly; investigation of the second was a principal purpose of my study, and it will be discussed in detail.

The association of the EP and crocodiles has long been noted, perhaps back to antiquity. Herodotus (Book 2, Ch. 68), who visited Egypt in 459 B.C., wrote of a bird called the Trochilos which entered the gaping mouths of basking crocodiles and picked leech-like parasites from the inside of their jaws. This story has been repeated and sometimes embellished by many later authors, both classical and modern. In the later versions, the bird has also been alleged to pick food particles from between the teeth. The fascination of Herodotus's account has endured. John Gould made a geographic exception in his "Birds of Asia" (1886, reprinted 1969) to include an artist's conception of EPs servicing the jaws of a gaping crocodile along the Nile, and even contemporary poets and novelists have used the tale to evoke an African atmosphere

(Kazantzakis, 1958, Book XII; Bellow, 1959, Ch. 5). The story of the Trochilos also spawned two long-lasting controversies over (1) whether any bird actually did this, and (2) if so, whether it was the EP or some other species such as one of the spur-winged plovers (*Hoplopterus* sp.). Herodotus did not describe the appearance of the bird, only its behavior, so the Trochilos could be identified only if one species alone were found to behave as recounted. The principal references on these points are Brehm (1879), Newton (1893-1896), Anderson (1898; reprinted 1965), Flower (1908), Koenig (1926), and Meinertzhagen (1959); the entire subject is reviewed in readable fashion by Guggisberg (1972) in his book on crocodiles. Brehm gave a colorful description of the EP-crocodile association and of the jaw-picking act, and wrote that he had seen this repeatedly. Newton was of the opinion that *Pluvianus* rather than *Hoplopterus* was the Trochilos of Herodotus on grounds that Brehm and others had seen *Pluvianus* jaw-picking whereas there was no reliable account of *Hoplopterus* doing this. Anderson, a herpetologist, thoroughly reviewed all references on the EP-crocodile relationship from Herodotus to his own time in impressive scholarly fashion. He doubted the jaw-picking stories and also refuted assertions that the EP was pictured in ancient Egyptian wall paintings and that its image was the basis for a hieroglyphic symbol. [After examining the extensive Egyptian collections in the British Museum, including excellently preserved coffin paintings of hieroglyphs and expertly depicted birds such as pratincoles (*Glareola* sp.), I fully agree with Anderson's conclusion.] Anderson's work was brought to the attention of ornithologists by Flower (1908), who also wrote that in many years of field experience with EPs and crocodiles he had never seen jaw-picking. Koenig never saw jaw-picking either, but he repeated the assertions of the symbolic importance of the EP in ancient Egypt, apparently unaware of Anderson's refutation. Meinertzhagen (1959) reviewed "the *Pluvianus*-Crocodile association" and wrote:

North of Khartoum I watched a large crocodile emerge from the river to a sandbank, flop down on its belly, close its eyes and open its jaws. Three *Pluvianus* who had been feeding near by at once flew to it, one perching on the outer gums and pecking at the teeth, the other two remaining on the ground and inspecting the mouth, occasionally reaching up and pecking the teeth; I could not say what was extracted by the birds but the whole episode looked as though the crocodile expected and invited the birds, and the birds were quite at home inspecting the inside of the mouth of the crocodile.

After quoting a similar account from a correspondent, Meinertzhagen then cites his own observation "on the Bafue River in north-west Rhodesia in 1907" where, in response to the presence of basking, gaping crocodiles, "the spur-winged plover (*Hoplopterus armatus*) would come flying in, sometimes from a long distance, and at once run up to the open jaws and pick teeth, though I never saw a bird actually enter the jaws." Although much detail is given, the lack of specific dates and precise localities makes it uncertain whether Meinertzhagen based these accounts on records written at the time or to a large extent on memory of events long past. Also, despite his vast field experience, Meinertzhagen sometimes made specific positive assertions that are demonstrably wrong (Cade and Maclean, 1967). Cott (1961) cites observations reported to him of birds other than *Pluvianus* picking crocodiles' teeth, but provides no new information on the EP.

On the basis of the published evidence, I conclude that (1) EPs probably sometimes pick food from jaws and teeth of crocodiles, perhaps even entering the open mouth; (2) this activity may have been more frequent and widespread in earlier times, when both crocodiles and EPs were common all along the Nile; (3) spur-winged plovers and other species may also pick crocodiles' teeth; (4) it is impossible to identify with certainty the Trochilos of Herodotus; and (5) the EP was not used as a symbol by the ancient Egyptians. Suffice it to say that, in the modern era at least, pickings from crocodiles' jaws do not constitute a major source of food for the EP. I myself never saw crocodile jaw-picking by the EP or by any other bird during two and a half months of observation.

The name *Trochilus* (Latin spelling) was inappropriately used by Linnaeus for a genus of hummingbirds (Trochilidae), a usage that is retained because of the law of priority in the rules of nomenclature. The probable explanation for Linnaeus' apparent error is reviewed by Newton (1893-1896: 442).

Of greater biological interest than the EP-crocodile relationship are reports of egg burial by the EP and the relation of this to incubation by solar heat. These two subjects—egg burial and thermoregulation—should be considered separately. Brehm (1854) was the first biologist to report that the EP buries its eggs. He found only one nest, and later described his discovery at length in his popular "Thierleben" (1879). Von Heuglin (1873) cited Brehm's first report but stated that he himself had always found the eggs lying in the open. Von Heuglin's account, which lacks detail, has not been confirmed by any later investigator and he presumably found abandoned eggs or mistook the eggs of some other species for those of the EP. Seebohm (1888) quoted extensively from the reports of Capt. W. W. C. Verner and Lt. G. Verner, who made observations along the Nile in Sudan in 1884-1885; they found EP eggs largely or completely buried (Seebohm was evidently quoting a letter, for I have not been able to find any publication by the Verners between 1885 and 1888 [or later] that includes this material). Koenig (1926) described finding single unburied eggs and buried EP clutches in Egypt in 1899, and he believed that the first egg was left unburied until the next one was laid. The only other firsthand published accounts of finding of EP nests with eggs are those of Ogilvie-Grant and Hawker (1902), Butler (1905), Hutson and Bannerman (1931), Jourdain and Schuel (1935), and Serle (1939). Although the accounts differ in some details, all agree that the eggs are kept largely or completely buried during the day, that an attending parent might or might not uncover the eggs to some extent before settling, and that the bird almost always covers the eggs with additional sand as it leaves the nest. All these accounts are based on brief observations, usually lasting little more than the time required to find the eggs.

The adaptive value of the egg-burying was presumed to be related to concealment but especially to incubation. Most observers noted the extreme heat at unshaded nest sites and suggested that burying the eggs might function to protect them from the sun. This implied that the nest and eggs were exposed to solar heat through lack of attendance by the parents. W. W. C. Verner (quoted by Seebohm, 1888) seems first to have suggested this when he reported his impression that the adult birds spent little or no time on the nest ". . . as if there were no such thing as the responsibilities and duties of incubation." Koenig (1926) cited an oral suggestion by Moebius in 1899 that burying the eggs protected them from extreme solar heat and that heat retained by the sand might help to warm the eggs at night. Koenig was evidently impressed with this idea and passed it on to Rey (1899), adding that temperatures of the surface of the sand where EPs nest might exceed 60°C. This is the only published temperature figure pertaining to the nest of the EP (twentieth century editions of Brehm's "Tierleben" cite

Rey as the authority for this figure, but Rey made clear that he was quoting information directly from Koenig).

The cumulative effect of all these accounts created an impression that the EP did little or no incubating but left its buried eggs to be incubated by solar heat, a situation similar to that found within the galliform family Megapodidae. Stresemann (1927-1934), after noting that incubation by environmental heat is known only in two groups of birds (the megapodes and, among waders, Pluvianus alone), wrote of the EP that (translation):

> It buries its clutch about 10 cm deep in hot sand of stream-islands and leaves it there for solar heat to incubate. The only brood care that it seems to put forth until the hatching of the young, consists therein, that it sits and covers the eggs in the hottest part of the day, perhaps, to lessen the effects of the solar radiation (Koenig, 1926).

This statement goes considerably beyond what Koenig actually wrote. Apart from mentioning that burying the eggs may serve to protect them from extreme solar heat, Koenig's discussion was devoted mostly to establishing that burial of the eggs is the usual, natural condition and not just the consequence of alarm reactions.

Stresemann's unequivocal tone and his enormous authority were doubtless responsible for statements in subsequent compilations, reviews, and textbooks that the EP buries its eggs and leaves them to be incubated by solar heat. This was stated, for example, by Skutch (1957), who cited Kendeigh (1952), who cited Stresemann (1927-1934), who had cited an original observer (Koenig) but had significantly extended his conclusions. Yet Stresemann only concluded firmly from the available data what others had implied. The problem was that there were no continuous, long-term observations of nest-attendance by the parents and practically no temperature measurements, both of which were essential to settling the questions about the incubation strategy of the EP.

G. Verner was the first and only observer to date to record wetting of the eggs by the parent birds, which is done by soaking their ventral feathers in the river and returning to sit on the buried eggs. His accurate description (quoted by Seebohm, 1888) was apparently ignored by all later authors except Knowlton (1909).

Percival (1906) was the first to report finding a young EP buried in the sand, but Butler (1931) first provided detailed descriptions of adults burying chicks in and away from the nest. Butler also reported that an adult EP drank water and regurgitated it on a buried chick. This unique observation has been quoted in almost all subsequent accounts of the nesting of the EP.

As shown by this cursory review, all of the published (and sometimes conflicting) information on the remarkable reproductive behavior of the EP is based on the original observations of eight or nine people from the latter part of the nineteenth century up to and no later than 1939. It is no slight to the integrity and accuracy of those authors to point out that their data on the breeding of the EP were based on brief encounters and that their accounts were largely anecdotal.

As a consequence of my long-term interest in avian adaptations that contribute to reproductive success in difficult and unusual environments, I undertook an investigation of the reproductive biology of the EP in the hope of providing detailed and quantitative information that would shed light on many of the unresolved questions about its behavior. In subsequent sections I will discuss all of the previous findings cited above in the context of my own observations.

THE STUDY AREA AND LOCAL CONDITIONS

I studied the EP in the field at Gambela, elevation 450 m, Ilubabor Province, Ethiopia, from 24 January to 6 April 1977. All of my observations of the EP were made at that place during that time, and my generalizations are based largely or entirely on those observations. I realize that such generalizations may not necessarily apply to individuals or populations of EPs at other places or at other times.

Gambela is a village on the north bank of the Baro River at latitude 8°15′N, longitude 34°38′E. In this region the river flows generally east to west and its waters eventually drain into the Nile. During the rainy season the Baro overflows into adjacent lowlands, but from December to May (during the dry season) the water level declines greatly and the river is largely contained within steep banks. At this time existing islands expand and many new ones appear. Some are entirely of rock but others include relatively flat areas of sand, silt, and gravel and may support some coarse grasses, herbaceous weeds, canes, and shrubs. During my stay the water level generally continued to decline from January to April, but there were some temporary rises caused by rains in the highlands to the east. There were no sustained rains in the vicinity of Gambela, and occasional thunderstorms there had no obvious effect on the river level. Even at lowest levels the water remained somewhat turbid and the bottom was not visible below a depth of about 0.7 m. Very few islands included patches of fine white sand; in most cases the substrate was pale to dark yellowish-brown, made up of coarse sand mixed with silt and gravel. On most islands the areas of gravel exceeded those of pure sand, and in some cases pure sand was found only in small patches.

The human population in the vicinity of Gambela numbers several thousand and most are of the Anuak and Nuer tribes, Nilotic people whose main sources of livelihood are fishing and farming. Fishing is done by spear, net, and hook and line, and most islands including those where EPs nest are visited daily by fishing people of all ages. The high ground along the riverbanks is planted with maize and sorghum, and around habitations bananas, papayas, and mangos are grown. At intervals along the edge of the river there are large fig (*Ficus sycamorus*), kapok (*Ceiba pentandra*), and sausage trees (*Kigelia pinnata*). These are used as lookout perches and nest sites by large birds including potential predators on the EP. Farther back from the river are wide expanses of tall grass, which are flooded during the wet season but which are burned during the dry season; beyond that, the habitat becomes dry forest and short grass savanna.

Trails and vehicle tracks run east and west of Gambela along the river, and almost all my field work was done on foot within 10 km in both directions from the town. I used dugouts to cross the river and to reach some islands; others could be reached by wading. Crocodiles were abundant, but only a few were large enough to be dangerous to humans and all were very wary on land and quickly slipped into the water if approached. Although the EP frequently associates closely with crocodiles in other parts of its range, I almost never saw the reptiles or the birds evidence any interest in each other. The EPs sometimes foraged within less than 1 m of basking crocodiles as though the latter were inanimate objects. Except for small terrestrial and arboreal lizards, other reptiles seemed very scarce in the dry season. Along the river I saw only one monitor lizard (*Varanus* sp.), a few small, slender water snakes, and no turtles. I found no evidence that the local reptiles had any influence on the nesting activity of the EP.

The river islands are regularly visited by a great variety of birds, and EPs react regularly and vigorously to the presence of those species that are potential predators or competitors. These visitors include herons (Ardeidae), storks (Scopidae and Ciconiidae), ibises (Threskiornithidae), raptors, especially Black Kite (*Milvus migrans;* hereafter "kite" refers only to this common species), African Fish Eagle (*Haliaeetus vocifer*), Hooded Vulture (*Necrosyrtes monachus*), African Harrier Hawk (*Polyboroides typus*), and Osprey (*Pandion haliaetus*); Wattled Plover (*Vanellus senegallus*); wintering Palaearctic shorebirds such as Greenshank (*Tringa nebularia*), Wood Sandpiper (*T. glareola*), Common Sandpiper (*T. hypoleucos*), and Little Stint (*Calidris minuta*); Black-winged Stilt (*Himantopus himantopus*); Striped (Senegal) Thick-knee (*Burhinus senegalensis*); various doves (Columbidae); Pied Crow (*Corvus albus*); the resident African Pied Wagtail (*Motacilla aguimp*), and the wintering Palaearctic White Wagtail (*M. alba*), and the Yellow Wagtail (*M. flava*).

The only mammal other than *Homo sapiens* that I saw in the river and on the islands was the hippopotamus (*Hippopotamus amphibius*). Hippos are scarce during the dry season near Gembela but the few individuals present are conspicuous. They had no evident influence on the EP but they might destroy a nest by stepping on it. If such destruction occurs it must be a rare accident, but a hippo track across one island came within a few meters of an EP nest site. At least one species of partly diurnal mongoose (Viverridae, unidentified) is fairly common around Gambela and would be a potentially dangerous predator if it went to the islands, but I found no evidence (sightings, tracks, scats) that it does. Thus, the river islands used for nesting by the EP are apparently free of all but aerial predators and man. In my experience the local people had little or no knowledge of the nesting habits of the EP and no interest in seeking its small eggs for food, but unintentional and persistent disturbance of breeding EPs by people on the islands appeared to cause some nesting failures.

GENERAL NATURAL HISTORY

In the following sections I attempt to summarize observations on the natural history of the EP, especially those relevant to its breeding biology. Detailed data on incubation temperatures and egg weight loss are treated separately but in the context provided by this general account. Most analyses of behavior and comparisons with other studies of the EP and other relevant species are given in the Discussion section.

ACTIVITIES INDEPENDENT OF BREEDING

FEEDING BEHAVIOR OF ADULTS

The EP appears to feed mainly on arthropods, particularly on insects. It is a versatile forager that obtains prey by methods as diverse as sand-probing and catching flying insects on the run, and this versatility is an important factor in the success of the species. The EP is superficially plover-like in morphology, with a short but pointed bill. It may walk slowly with frequent pauses for searching, or run rapidly to catch prey sighted at a distance. The EP readily wades into quiet water, but unless bathing or soaking (see subsequent sections) almost never ventures deeper than about the distal half of the tarsometatarsus and for feeding does not put its head in the water beyond the base of the bill. Most of its foraging is done above the water line on the sand-silt-gravel substrate of the islands, but at times it forages along the river banks or goes beyond them into cut-over fields and around native huts.

Surface picking.

The EP often walks along and captures small prey at the substrate surface by visual searching and quick use of the bill. Small plants growing sparsely in an expanse of sand may be carefully searched for arthropods. Sometimes an EP will suddenly run in a straight course for many meters and seize an insect from the substrate at the end of its run; the bird appears to have spied the prey at a distance and to have gone directly after it. Rarely, the EP will stalk a winged insect at rest. In this activity the bird's behavior resembles that of a stalking heron. The foreparts are lowered, the hindquarters are tilted up, the head is slightly drawn back, and the EP creeps forward slowly and steadily, its eyes fixed on the prey. When it is within range, the insect is seized with a quick thrust of the bill.

Fly-catching.

This method is used infrequently and opportunistically when there are low-flying insects about. The EP runs rapidly and erratically, apparently tracking and catching the flying insects. The bird's wings may be slightly spread during the run, but it does not break into flight. Rarely, the EP flashes the largely white surface of its wings by partly spreading and raising them, in a manner similar to that of New World mockingbirds (*Mimus* sp.). In the case of the EP, this appears to serve only to flush insects which are then pursued.

Sand-probing.

This activity is similar to that of many other small charadriiform birds foraging in damp sand. The EP walks along or runs in short bursts, stopping to probe with the full length of its bill. The EP may also excavate by tossing sand to either side with lateral flicks of the bill. Holes several times deeper than the length of the bill are excavated this way.

Jump-scratching.

This foraging method seems similar to that described for some other glareolids. The EP jumps forward and scratches backward on damp sand, usually after a short run. The feet are brought far anteriorly during the jump and sand is thrust forward on the impact of landing as the toes dig in. At once the bird draws both feet backward simultaneously, throwing a spray of sand to the rear and exposing small prey. The action is curiously reminiscent of that of some American emberizines (Fringillidae), which scratch with both feet simultaneously in leaf litter. I do not recall seeing EPs jump-scratching in dry sand, presumably because this substrate lacks concealed prey.

Stone-turning.

This foraging method is apparently the same as that used by turnstones (*Arenaria* sp.) and is frequently and regularly used by EPs. The bird walks over gravelly substrate, using the bill to flip over stones either in an anterior or lateral direction; exposed prey is then seized. I weighed stones that I estimated to be the same size as the largest ones turned by EPs and they were about 70 g, slightly less than the body weight of the bird. Not only stones but debris of all kinds—leaves, cane stalks, driftwood—are turned over in the same way.

Drinking.

To drink, the EP goes to or into shallow water, puts its bill in vertically or nearly so, withdraws it after at most one second, and brings the head up to a horizontal position. This may be repeated several times with pauses of several seconds between drinks. While immersed, the bill is never raised so as to cup water in the lower mandible, nor is the head tilted above horizontal in swallowing. The contrast of the EP's drinking posture with the awkward scooping motions of some of the ciconiiform and raptorial birds was striking. Drinking by the EP occurs most often during the hottest parts of the day but is neither frequent nor prolonged. I doubt that an EP spends a total of more than one minute per day in drinking, and it is difficult to see how the bird could take in anything more than a few drops of water per drink. Chicks of all ages, even on the day of hatching, may go to the water and drink in the same manner as adults.

BODY MAINTENANCE AND COMFORT ACTIVITIES

Preening.

The movements of the EP in preening are similar to those of most other charadriiform birds, and I did not notice any unusual or unique features. EPs often preen while sitting on the nest, particularly during the hot hours.

Face-cleaning.

Sand-probing and stone-turning often result in accumulation of sand on the feathers around the base of the bill. This sand is removed by tilting the head down and to one side and scratching with the toenails of a raised foot. Unlike most other coursers, the EP does not have a pectinate middle toenail; instead, the nail is expanded medially to form a curved flange. Foot-scratching is direct, not over the wing, and I did not see this action used to clean any parts of the plumage except the anterior facial area. Chicks as young as the day of hatching may also show this behavior. Direct scratching is characteristic of coursers but not of true plovers (Jehl, 1975).

Bathing.

This is done in the usual charadriiform manner. The EP wades in, dips its head in and out of the water, then droops and shakes the wings as the body rocks from side to side. Even recently-hatched chicks may bathe in essentially this same way.

Wing-stretching.

This is rarely done. The bird crouches down to the substrate, leans to one side, and then extends one wing for about one second. Usually the other wing is not stretched immediately or even soon afterward.

Gaping.

This is done rarely and apparently randomly, either while standing anywhere or while sitting on the nest. The bill is briefly opened to an angle of about 30° and some kinesis of the upper mandible is evident. The mouth lining is black like the rest of the bill, and I did not see a gape directed at another bird. It appears to be a comfort movement, like yawning, without special social significance.

Standing on one foot.

After running or walking on land or in water, the EP often pauses with one leg half-flexed for several seconds in a graceful pose. The leg is not withdrawn out of sight into the ventral feathers, nor does the bird ever hop along on one foot as do some of the sandpipers (Scolopacidae). In the EP, this stance appears to be a comfort posture while maintaining readiness to move on.

Responses to heat stress.

Incubation and brooding expose adult birds to full sun during the hottest hours of the day. At such times the dorsal plumage is elevated to varying degrees but only rarely to an extreme. The wings are not noticeably drooped nor are the head and neck feathers conspicuously raised, but the elongate black interscapular feathers may be elevated well above the level of others on the dorsum (pl. 3). Although conspicuous, these feathers were not raised or spread in any of the EP's displays that I saw. When elevated by a sitting bird, these black feathers would absorb some solar heat that would otherwise penetrate to the bird's body surface; the absorbed heat could then be dissipated by convection (Walsberg, Campbell, and King, 1978). The area potentially protected from heat-loading by this means is small but lies right in the mid-dorsal line. Protection of the underlying spinal cord from excessive external heating may be of special importance, for the cord (in pigeons) has been shown to contain thermosensitive structures that are involved in thermoregulatory responses to changes in core temperature (Rautenberg et al., 1972). The bird may pant by opening the bill to an extent of about 3 mm at the tip; respiratory movements are visible but not conspicuous, and there is definitely no gular flutter. The inner surface of the bill glistens with moisture but the tongue is not noticeably raised. There is no visible discharge from the nostrils and no salt crust around them that would indicate an active nasal salt-excreting gland (a white crust would show clearly on the black bill). As the birds live only along rivers

Activities Related to Breeding

ATTAINMENT OF BREEDING CONDITION

When I arrived in Gambela during the last week of January, most EPs were paired and a few already had eggs. The earliest date of egg-laying for which I have evidence was about the first or second week of January, calculated from the fact that one pair had juveniles approximately three weeks old on 27 February. At the latitude of Gambela the day length (sunrise to sunset) is about 11.6 hours at the winter solstice on 21 December and increases only about five minutes by the last week of January. This slight change suggests that gonadal growth is not initiated by an increase in photoperiod but may be regulated by an endogenous cycle, or by environmental factors other than photoperiod, or by some combination of these. The low water level of the dry season is essential for successful nesting of the EP and its breeding condition must coincide with this period, but suggestions of specific environmental timers of reproduction can only be speculative. As the EP lives at the water's edge, any direct effect (such as physiological dehydration) of general environmental dryness can presumably be ruled out, but numerous indirect effects are possible. Among these might be changes in the availability of abundance of certain kinds of food, or the exposure of previously-flooded nesting substrates. As the dry season is of regular annual occurrence, an endogenous annual rhythm of reproductive activity that coincided appropriately with that season would be favored by selection. Perhaps there is an annual endogenous rhythmicity subject to adjustments in timing by effects of the dry season on local environmental conditions.

The literature on the EP records formation of flocks during the high-water nonbreeding season, but there are no recorded observations of early stages of pair formation. At Gambela in late January up to six EPs sometimes gathered at a few favored foraging spots, but these groups intermittently sorted out into pairs, showed intragroup aggression, and never formed a close flock. Most EPs were paired, attempting to defend territories, and commencing nest-scraping activities before 1 February. I saw nothing that I could interpret as preliminary courtship or pairing behavior in advance of territoriality and nest-scrapemaking, and if the species shows overt behavior of a more preliminary kind it remains to be described.

TAMENESS

The literature includes many references to the EP as being unwary of humans, tame, or even extremely tame. This is undoubtedly the case at some times and places, but birds of my study population were not especially tame and were about as wary as small plovers that inhabit beaches frequented by people. Sometimes I was approached to within 1 m by a foraging EP as I sat quietly on a sandbar, but usually they seemed acutely aware of being watched and would run off or fly away if I attempted to approach them closely, usually within about 10 m. I attribute this degree of wariness to the physiological state of the birds in the breeding season and not to local circumstance, for the people of Gambela paid no attention to the EPs and never molested them.

VOCALIZATIONS

The EP is highly vocal during the breeding season but it does not have a greatly varied repertoire. Both sexes have identical voices. The most frequent vocalization is a series of rapid, harsh notes, usually uttered as the bird flies in pursuit of another EP or some other species. These notes may be approximated phonetically as "cherk-cherk-cherk...." or "chur-chur-chur...." The number of such notes per burst is seldom less than three and may continue many times more but not necessarily for any particular number. The tempo and amplitude are not always regular, but one often hears a pattern of progressively rising then diminishing amplitude. I could detect no difference in these calls when given during either intra- or interspecific conflicts. Such calls, which I designate the "cherk-series," are given in conflict situations (the approach of a conspecific territorial intruder or of a potential predator or competitor) and usually accompany an aggressive charge or pursuit by the EP. The cherk-series seems primarily to augment the effect of the EP's aggressive charge rather than to serve as a threat that may substitute for it. Intra- or interspecific visual threat displays are usually accompanied initially by strident incisive clucks (see below), but these may be succeeded by a cherk-series if threatening circumstances persist. Sometimes an EP may give a cherk-series while remaining on the nest or elsewhere in the territory, or it may give a cherk-series as it flies out of its territory to forage, without any apparent conflict stimulus. The sonogram in figure 1a represents a portion of a cherk-series recorded as I (a potential predator) closely approached an EP nest.

An apparently intra-specific vocal communication combines an initial "wheep" or "wheeup" note (see below) followed at once by a variable number of cherks, usually three to five, "wheep! cherk-cherk-cherk." I heard this call given only within the calling bird's territory, usually when its mate was in sight but not close or apparently when the mate might be within range of hearing if not actually in sight. This vocalization appears to signal the presence of a bird to its mate and possibly to indicate a readiness to interact with the mate in some way. Such a call from one bird is not answered with a call by the mate, but the mate often comes close to the caller shortly afterward. For example, an incubating or brooding bird might give this call and then soon be approached by its mate for a change-over. Most change-overs, though, took place without any vocal signals. In another example, an EP alone in a small territory might give this call, then be joined by its mate that had been foraging elsewhere, and then itself leave to forage. Put verbally, the call seems to say "mate-I-am-here." This may stimulate the mate to approach and to relieve the calling bird from nest attendance or territorial defense.

In the vicinity of the nest site, EPs may give notes that I call "clucks" of different intensities. Even at low intensity these sounds have a plangent quality that suggests to me the term "incisive clucks" (fig. 1b). Low-intensity or "soft" incisive clucks are sometimes given by members of a pair during nest scrape-making, and in this circumstance the clucks are given in a series of three to six at a rate of about two per second. The sounds are produced with the bill apparently closed and it is difficult to discern which of two birds is vocalizing or if both are, but some instances of overlap show that both

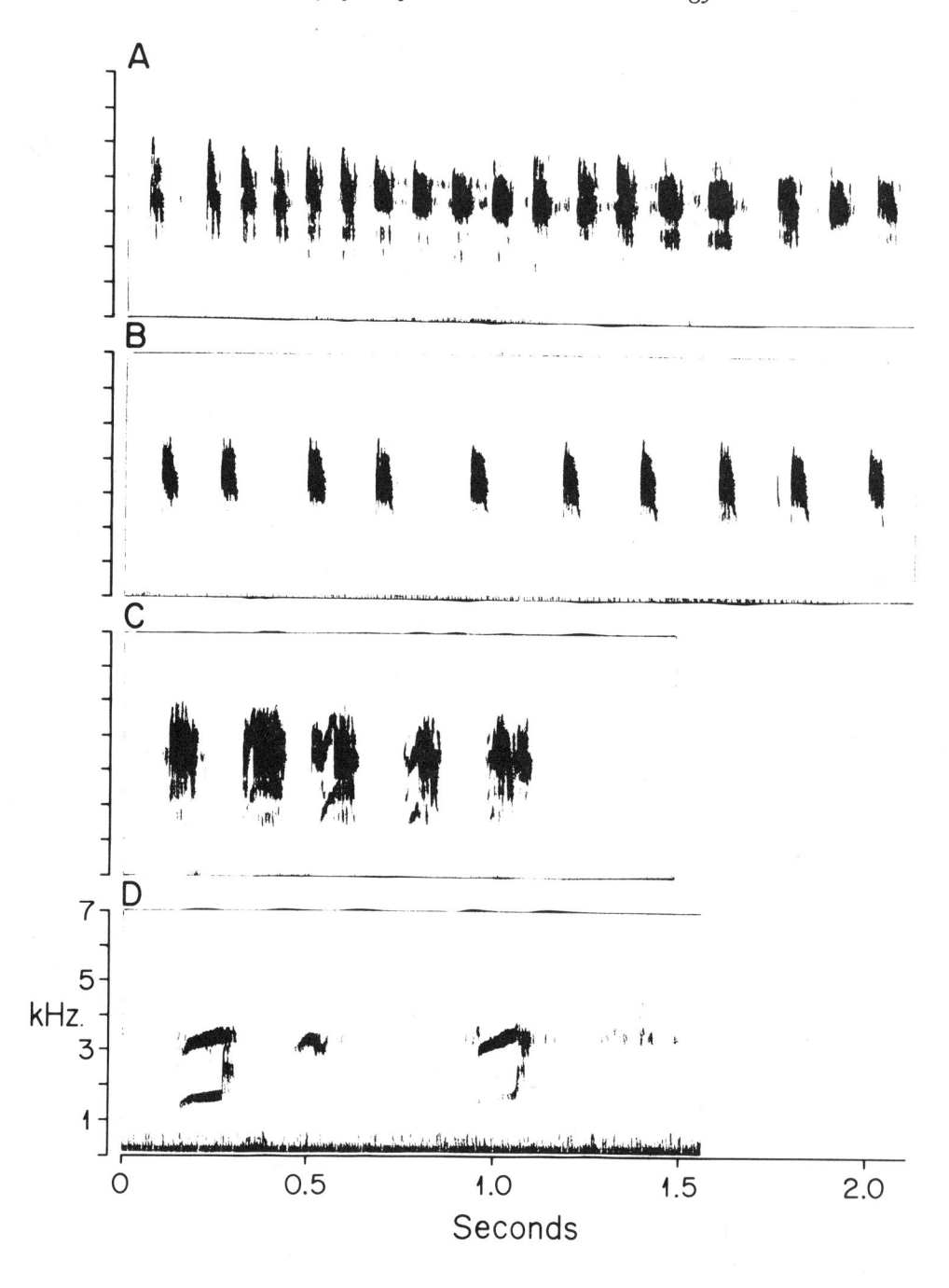

Fig. 1. Sonograms of vocalizations of *Pluvianus aegyptius:* (a) the cherk series; (b) incisive clucks; (c) strident incisive clucks; (d) the wheep note. See text for discussion.

produce the same sounds. A higher-intensity incisive cluck is given by parents attending newly-hatched chicks or eggs in late stages of incubation when potential predators are in the vicinity although not approaching aggressively. An even higher-intensity sound that I call the "strident incisive cluck" (fig. 1c) is directed toward predators closely approaching the nest and accompanies distraction displays and wing-waving threat displays. During the two higher-intensity vocalizations the bill is conspicuously opened. I interpret the incisive cluck as indicating a general condition of agitation by birds close to their nest site, given at low intensity in the presence of a mate and at progressively higher intensities as a predator poses an increasing threat. I do not believe that hostility toward the mate is indicated by the low-intensity call; by the time the pair is involved in scrape-making, the pair bond seems firmly established and there are no overt signs of aggression between the two birds.

A note that I represent phonetically as "wheep" or "wheeup" (fig. 1d) is given either singly or repeatedly (but never in rapid, regular sequence) by adult birds, most often when they are with chicks out of the nest but sometimes at earlier nesting stages with unhatched eggs. To my ear this call is more melodious than any of the others although not strikingly so. The wheep note is often uttered without perceptible opening of the bill but sometimes the bill is opened slightly. This note seems usually to signal a distant alert that is perceptible to the mate or chicks or both. For example, if I walked in the direction of a sandbar where chicks were out foraging, one of the parent birds would probably start giving wheep calls as soon, presumably, as my steady progress in that direction was noticed, which might be up to 100 m away. The adult birds did not seem to exchange calls nor did adults or chicks show any specific alarm behavior in response. These calls carry well but the point of source is difficult to locate. My impression is that they serve as a "first stage alert" that persists as long as the potential predator is around but that changes to other responses in case of closer and more threatening approach. The wheep note seems to be used only in association with large potential predators, not with conspecific intruders or other competitors.

The structure of the different notes as shown by the sonograms supports the aural impression that vocalizations of the EP are not greatly varied. I suggest that there is a graded series from the lower to higher-intensity incisive clucks to cherk notes. A sound similar to the wheep note seems to merge into the incisive cluck to produce a more strident quality (fig. 1c), and this may be succeeded by the cherk note as the bird's agitation increases. The cherk note in series seems to be the ultimate vocalization associated with high levels of agitation, whether generated by intra- or interspecific intrusions into the territory or by threat of predation. The cluck notes seem to signify lower levels of agitation at close range, and the wheep note is a relatively distant general alert, used among the pairs or in a family group. When the wheep note (alerting the mate) is followed by a short series of cherks (indicating strong agitation) to form the "mate-I-am-here" signal, this seems to bring an approach by the mate and some action that relieves the agitation.

INDIVIDUAL RECOGNITION

My original intention was to capture and mark EPs with colored rings for individual identification. I did not attempt this initially as I was extremely cautious about disturbing the birds and possibly disrupting the normal sequence of events of nesting.

Such cautiousness was probably unnecessary, but I later decided that capture and marking, although desirable, did not seem essential in view of the birds' behavior. After monitoring the activities of both members of various pairs for many days and many continuous hours, I could detect no qualitative difference in the behavior of the two individuals at any stage throughout the breeding cycle. This statement is based on observations when both members of a pair were simultaneously in view, or when one replaced the other at the nest and then through many subsequent change-overs. Indeed, apart from the necessarily differing roles in copulation and egg-laying, the EP seems to come as close to sexual monomorphism as is possible for a dioecious vertebrate species. There is no known external morphological difference, and sexual identity of captured live birds could in most cases be determined only by laparotomy. Possibly one sex or the other is in attendance at the nest more often at certain times, but even if so there is no qualitative difference in their behavior. Sometimes individuals of a pair could be distinguished temporarily by slight adventitious plumage differences, but otherwise they appeared (and sounded) identical. How the birds recognize each other individually I do not know. They obviously do so at considerable distances, as is shown by frequent immediate attacks by one member of a pair on any intruder into the nesting territory at times when the mate is away. The absent mate may then return and join in the fracas. I never saw an EP start to attack another which then turned out to be its mate.

NESTING SITES

The EP requires a site with sufficient sand to make a nest scrape and to cover its eggs. Rarely it may nest with no more than that, but usually a pair chooses a site with enough deep, loose sand to cover the eggs easily. On a larger scale, the EP seems to nest only on islands and not on peninsulae. There were several large peninsulae on which EPs regularly foraged and even made some nest scrapes, but I found no nests with eggs on any of these. Some islands with nests remained insular at lowest water levels only by channels as little as 1 m wide and 0.1 m deep, but none became connected with the mainland above water. The avoidance of otherwise suitable sandy areas that were not islands was striking. Eggs were sometimes laid on islands that were probably too small to support chicks safely and such nesting attempts ultimately failed.

TERRITORIALITY

During the breeding season the EP is intensely territorial and aggressive, invariably so intraspecifically and usually so toward potential predators and toward all other birds that are potential competitors for food. Around its nest site the EP is boldly aggressive against a variety of avian species of many sizes, and some of these birds appear baffled by the vigorous displays and attacks of the EPs. Local species that are attacked when they invade EP territories include all ciconiiform birds, all raptors, most charadriiforms, all doves, Pied Crows, and all wagtails. Of these, some of the ciconiiforms may be potential predators on chicks if not eggs, and several raptors are potential predators on EPs at any stage from egg to adult. Pied Crows probably take eggs and young chicks. The charadriiforms are usually potential competitors for food as are the doves and the wagtails, both of which are surface foragers on the sand-gravel bars. Only a few species of doves visit the islands and usually come only to drink, but wagtails commonly forage for insects there and are invariably attacked and driven off by territorial EPs. Kingfishers (Alcedinidae) and bee-eaters (Meropidae) are not chased even though they forage around or over the islands and occasionally perch within an EP territory, although usually not on the sand.

Much of the interspecific aggression is directed against species which are probably not potential predators or serious competitors for food. The Sacred Ibis (*Threskiornis aethiopica*) is one such species that is a frequent visitor into EP territories, and the ibises are vigorously and persistently attacked. The greenshank almost always forages while wading in water too deep for EPs and probably takes nothing that would be available to the latter, yet EPs often seem especially aggressive toward greenshanks and sometimes fly at them from at least 100 m away. On the other hand, stilts are almost never attacked although they appear more likely competitors for food than the greenshanks. Some raptors such as the Long-crested Eagle (*Lophoaetus occipitalis*) come rarely to the islands to drink or bathe and probably pose no threat to the EPs, but these are also attacked.

The EPs show different degrees of readiness to attack that seem to correspond roughly to the degree of danger or competition represented by the intruder. Highest priority is given to other EPs, followed by kites and Pied Crows equally, and then wagtails. Evidently selection has favored a high level of aggressiveness toward actual predators and competitors, and this behavior "spills over" in many cases to other species that seldom or never pose a serious threat. The intensity of the alarm and aggressive response to kites has been somewhat puzzling to me. Kites are abundant around Gambela; the air is always full of them during the daytime, soaring high and low everywhere, and in the hot hours they alight on the islands to drink and bathe. The kite is a tireless and bold forager and certainly a potential predator on the EP, but it largely scavenges around Gambela and I have never seen one attempt to capture a live bird of any kind. Nevertheless, EPs always show great alarm at the close approach of a kite and usually attack one if it alights within the EPs' territory. The attacks involve not only high intensity displays and vocalizations, but also actual strikes on the kite (pl. 4), and the latter is often pursued as high as 50 m into the air and struck from behind as it flies away. Yet at no time have I seen a kite show predatory interest in the EP—adults, eggs, or young.

The Pied Crow is regarded with equal alarm and aggressiveness, and with good reason. They use the tall kapok trees along the riverbank as lookout perches and nest sites and command a sweeping view of many of the islands where EPs nest. The crows often soar in thermals and then descend rapidly if a foraging opportunity develops. They also come to the islands to drink and bathe, and territorial EPs attack them vigorously. The crows sometimes counter-attack with advances and bill-jabs, and they often respond to the EPs' agitation by walking about and thrusting their bills into the sand, tossing it sideways, apparently seeking buried eggs or chicks of the EP. This seems to be random searching and I have not seen the crows discover any nests this way, but at least one nest in which I found punctured and empty egg-shells was probably raided by crows and perhaps they also take nonflying young birds. As in the case of kites, EPs often pursue and strike crows high in the air, and the harassments by the EPs are usually effective although they probably could inflict no real damage.

SIZE OF THE TERRITORY

Each pair of EPs attempts to secure an entire island, regardless of size, as its territory and is usually successful. On only two islands did I find two pairs of nesting EPs; each of the other fourteen active nests that I found was the only one present on the island. As islands are usually of irregular shape it is difficult to estimate their areas, but some on which EPs nested were at least several thousand m² in extent. The smallest was a rock island about 15 m x 3 m with a patch of sand covering about 3 m². The nest on this small island was apparently destroyed by a predator and the site was abandoned. Some of the larger islands had only relatively small areas of sand suitable for EP nesting, so the resident did not face vigorous territorial challenges for much of the space; nevertheless, intruding EPs foraging on any part of the island were usually attacked and driven off as soon as detected. If, however, the sand contours or vegetation patches put part of an island out of sight of an established EP territory, another pair might secure a territory on the same island. I saw this happen on one island, and the second pair to gain a territory had a nest site which could not be seen from the site of the first pair. Along the river's edge birds of each pair met while foraging, and after frequent conflicts it appeared that each pair effectively defended a territory extending 15 m in any direction from its nest site. In many other instances of territorial defense it also appeared that about 15 m from the nest was a critical distance at which EPs would usually stand and fight if others attempted a closer intrusion. If threat displays or charges were effective at greater distances, as they often were, a pair would defend a much larger area. Following the subsequent section on aggressive displays, I describe a specific case of territorial conflict and its outcome.

ALERT AND AGGRESSIVE DISPLAYS

Alert posture.

This posture is assumed by an EP when it appears to notice another animal with which it may interact. The feathers are generally compressed, the neck is extended vertically, the head may be horizontal or tilted slightly above that level, and the body is either horizontal or angled so that the foreparts are raised and the tail lowered (pl. 5). In the most extreme (high-intensity) form of this posture, the bird's head-neck-body axis may be inclined about 60° above horizontal and the foreparts may be bobbed up and down while the hindparts may remain relatively stationary. The short feathers of the forehead are usually fully raised, temporarily giving the appearance of a small frontal crest. In the less extreme (low-intensity) form of this posture, the bird simply looks sleeked and alert. In the latter case in particular, the bird may bob its foreparts up and down in the manner of many other charadriiform species. In most circumstances there is no vocalization, but a wheep note may be given if young birds are involved in the situation (see Vocalizations).

Looking-up.

This activity is so frequent and conspicuous among EPs that it deserves special mention. EPs are constantly on the alert for aerial predators, especially during the hottest parts of the day when soaring conditions are best, and EPs at or near a nest look up at the sky every few minutes. An EP on a nest, for example, frequently turns its head laterally through 90° so that one eye is directed straight up into the sky and often into the sun (pl. 3). If the sun is not more or less overhead, the bird turns its head one way and then the other so that it looks away from and into the sun, never seeming to avoid it and perhaps looking into it more often than not. Looking-up is not just a fleeting glance but a well-defined activity pattern that presumably serves an important function. Aerial predator detection must be one such function, as sitting EPs are always conspicuous and would inevitably reveal the exact location of the nest if they did not leave whenever danger approaches. In addition, after seeing EPs look up at the sun once or several times before soaking themselves and then wetting the eggs, I began to suspect that they might be checking the position of the sun and perhaps the intensity of its radiation. I have no definite evidence for this supposition but feel that it deserves further consideration in future investigations. As expected, Looking-up often accompanies Alert posture but it may also occur in birds sitting low on the nest or while approaching it when there are no obvious indications of danger.

Moderate Fluff.

If an intraspecific interaction develops toward an aggressive encounter in which neither bird readily retreats, an EP may go into a Moderate Fluff. In this posture the body and head are horizontal, the neck is not noticeably extended, and the ventral feathers are fluffed out; there may be slight dorsal fluffing. This posture may be assumed while frontally facing another EP, approached or approaching, even to within 0.5 m; the fluffed bird stands still, and there is no vocalization. The effect is to make the bird look bigger and it may serve as an intimidation posture.

Hunched Run.

An aggressive EP may charge an adversary (intra- or interspecific) in a Hunched Run. This posture is similar to that seen in many gulls (*Larus* sp.). The body is horizontal, the head is lowered to a level even with or lower than the back but parallel to it, the bill is directed forward, and the bird runs toward the adversary. Apparently, the higher the agitation, the lower the level of the head. No vocalization is given. A Hunched Run usually routs any smaller species of bird, some larger ones, and any EPs intruding within an established territory.

Threat Displays.

When a Hunched Run does not result in the quick retreat of an adversary, or if suddenly confronted by a potential predator or an aggressive conspecific intruder, an EP may exhibit more striking posture. The largely white remiges with a sharply defined black stripe are used importantly in high-intensity Threat Displays. Such displays are somewhat different when directed against intra- or interspecific adversaries. Each display is usually used only in the respective context, but occasionally the birds shifts from one into the other in situations of great stress. Confronting another EP, the displaying bird tilts its foreparts down, raises its head, and almost instantaneously spreads its wings fully while tilting them forward so that their plane is almost vertical. The white-tipped tail is also cocked forward and slightly spread so that it forms a continuous contour with the wings. The visual effect is startling, like the sudden opening of a fan with a striking black and white pattern (pl. 1). The behavior is identical in both sexes, and the display may be accompanied by loud, strident vocalizations. The bird so confronted may respond with an identical display of its own. This type of display is most often seen in the earlier stages of the breeding cycle when territories are being secured or scrape-making is in progress, but it may be given at later stages as when an incubating EP is surprised by an intruder and gives this display as it rises from the nest.

The interspecific Threat Display also exposes the white-and-black pattern, but the spread wings are not tilted forward but extended laterally, drooped, and usually waved up and down slowly through an arc of about 20° (pls. 2, 6). The display is usually accompanied by strident incisive clucks followed by rapid, harsh cherk notes (see Vocalizations). I saw this display directed only against species larger than the EP, perhaps because only those did not flee at once when charged by an EP as did the smaller sandpipers and wagtails. During the late stages of incubation or when recently hatched chicks are present, this display is readily directed toward humans that closely approach the nest and remain close.

Once I was able to watch a successful displacement of an established pair of EPs by an invading pair and Threat Displays were conspicuously used. This conflict took place on an island of low relief about 200 m long, about 30 m wide at the widest, and about 1 m maximum elevation. Approximately two-thirds of this island was covered with gravel and with clumps of coarse grass, making that part unsuitable for EP nesting. I had observed the first pair making nest scrapes in numerous sites and defending the island with threats and attacks on wading birds, raptors, and other EPs. This pair did not have eggs and probably would not have had any for many more days. On the morning of 1 February, a second pair of EPs appeared on the same island and began scrape-making within 10 m to 15 m of the area where the first pair was active. The first pair vigorously challenged the intruders with charges and Threat Displays, but the intruding pair was highly aggressive and not only responded in the same manner but pressed its own attacks against the residents. Throughout the morning the contest continued with all four birds participating. Members of each pair made nest scrapes at particular sites as if this were a symbol of territorial dominance, and correspondingly the rival birds attempted to displace each other from their nest-scrape sites. A Hunched Run directed toward a scrape-making adversary might displace the latter, and the aggressor in this case might continue pursuit or pause to make a nest-scrape at the rival's site. Sometimes both members of a pair charged simultaneously in a Hunched Run, but usually the charges were done individually. If the bird at its nest-scrape site did not give way in response to a charge, the charging bird might run past and circle back, often confronting its adversary in a Moderate Fluff posture. Sometimes one member of each pair was at its own scrape site, each confronted by the other bird of the adversary pair. Aerial chases were frequent, but the birds soon returned to the island. When one bird pursued another on the sand the gap between them was usually about 1 m to 2 m, but such chases were sometimes surprisingly interrupted if the pursued bird suddenly stopped and began foraging. In that case the pursuer either ran past and turned back to attempt another charge, or it began foraging also. In this situation foraging seemed to be a displacement activity, similar to grass-pulling in gulls, that blunted aggressive conflict. In these two pairs, however, the territorial conflict was not resolved by ritualized actions.

Sometimes Threat Displays by opponents were followed by bill-grappling, flapping fights in which both birds tumbled over the sand and into shallow water where they continued to struggle. Despite vigorous defensive efforts by the first pair, the persistent aggressiveness and combative strength of the second pair prevailed and the first pair was ousted from the island by the end of the day. Circumstantial evidence suggested that the ousted pair then established a territory on a much smaller islet about 400 m away. The newly victorious pair subsequently maintained defense of the entire island and eventually laid a clutch of three eggs (table 1, 4a-c) and hatched two chicks.

Distraction Displays.

Although not part of territorial defense, these displays are performed only within the nesting territory and so are included here. If I approached closely and remained at or near a nest during the first three weeks of incubation, one or both adults might stay within a few meters, moving around and making false nest-scrapes or crouching and groveling with slightly drooping wings, gradually moving away from me. During later incubation stages or when chicks are hatched, the adults use a wider repertoire of displays. An adult bird may toss sand vigorously with lateral flicks of the bill, apparently simulating the uncovering of eggs or chicks, or it may make antero-posterior covering movements where no chick is present. In a more extreme form of groveling, the bird may feebly flap both slightly extended wings or lean on one side and feebly flap only one wing. It may then move away awkwardly with partly spread wings. This display is similar to the injury-feigning of many other charadriiform birds, and if the EP is followed it soon resumes its normal posture and run or fly away. If not followed, the bird may go into intense foraging activity, especially stone-turning, remaining close but moving slightly away from the intruder. EPs did not direct these distraction activities as often toward other birds as toward people; if other birds did not retreat before a threat display, the EPs usually charged and struck them. I was never struck, however, despite my persistent intrusions, nor did I see strikes at any other human intruder.

Landing Wing-raise.

Sometimes an EP comes in for a landing with legs dangling and wings fluttering and keeps the wings elevated momentarily after alighting, in the manner of many other charadriiform birds. This seems to maximize conspicuousness and contrasts with the usual landing in which the bird glides in low and closes the wings right after touching down. The Landing Wing-raise is usually or perhaps exclusively used when the mate or young birds are present. There is no special landing call and usually no vocalization accompanying the landing.

NESTING BEHAVIOR

SCRAPE-MAKING

This activity is one of the earliest and most persistent patterns of the reproductive cycle. With two pairs in which I was able to follow nesting events from the earliest establishment of a territory, Scrape-making continued for at least 30 days before

TABLE 1—Data from Eggs
Weights are in g, Linear Dimensions in mm. Group A: Eggs Left in
from Nests for Various Purposes. The Letters a, b, c Indicate Eggs of the

	Egg No.	Length (L)x breadth (B)	Wt. at first weighing	Est. days post-laying at first weighing	[Actual] or est. initial egg wt. (extrapolated)	[Actual] or est. initial egg wt. $W = K_w \cdot L \cdot B^2$	No. days between first and last weighing	No. of weighings	Total wt. loss
Group A	1a	32.0 x 24.1	9.691	13	10.185	10.174	6	2	0.237
	1b	33.4 x 24.0	9.681	12	10.125	10.488	6	2	0.224
	1c	33.9 x 23.4	9.440	11	9.836	10.161	6	2	0.215
	2	31.9 x 23.7	9.617	3	9.698	9.809	14	3	0.559
	3a	31.2 x 24.2	9.669	4	9.813	10.003	18	3	0.891
	3b	30.2 x 24.4	9.624	3	9.700	9.843	18	3	0.571
	4a	31.5 x 23.0	9.244	0	[9.244]	[9.244]	25.7	8	0.723
	4b	29.5 x 24.1	9.250	0	[9.250]	[9.250]	24.7	7	0.796
	4c	29.8 x 23.7	8.940	4	9.068	9.163	23	6	0.733
	5a*	29.6 x 23.0	8.510	0	[8.510]	[8.510]	5.3	2	0.177
	5b*	28.4 x 23.2	8.432	0	[8.432]	[8.432]	4.3	2	0.135
	$\bar{x}$								
Group B	5a*	—	—	—	—	—	16	12	0.948
	5b*	—	—	—	—	—	16	12	0.962
	6a	31.4 x 23.5	9.289	3	9.397	9.493	8	8	0.519
	6b	31.2 x 23.4	9.296	2	9.368	9.352	8	8	0.521
	7a	30.4 x 23.8	9.367	4	9.507	9.426	8	8	0.530
	8	32.0 x 24.2	9.874	3	9.985	10.260	17	13	1.198
Group C	7b	29.3 x 23.7	—	—	—	9.002			
	7c	29.4 x 23.5	—	—	—	8.720			
	9a	31.3 x 24.1	—	—	—	9.945			
	9b	30.7 x 24.1	—	—	—	9.754			
	$\bar{x}$	30.9 x 23.7			9.48	9.51			

*Same eggs; put in desiccator after abandonment in nest

of *Pluvianus aegyptius*
Nests; Group B: Eggs Placed in Desiccator; Group C: Eggs Removed
Same Clutch. See Text for Methods of Measurement, Definitions and Discussion.

$\dot{M}_{H_2O}$ $\bar{x}$ wt. loss · day^{-1}	Range of daily wt. loss	[Actual] or est. incubation period; days	Calculated F	Newly-hatched chick wt.		Shell thickness	Shell wt.
0.038	—	31	0.115	7.5			
0.037	—	30.5	0.111	7.4			
0.036	—	29	0.106	7.0			
0.040	0.027-0.047	[31]	0.128	7.4			
0.050	0.036-0.056	31	0.158	—			
0.032	0.025-0.035	30	0.100	—			
0.028	0.020-0.035	[31]	0.094	7.1			
0.032	0.030-0.040	[30]	0.100	7.0			
0.032	0.027-0.048	—	—	—		0.185	0.690
0.033	—	—	—	—		0.162	0.631
0.031	—	—	—	—		0.183	0.670
0.035		30.4	0.114	7.23			

	Adj. to 32 torr		Est. $\bar{T}_A$	Est. ΔP_{H_2O}, torr	G_{H_2O} (conductance)	$\dfrac{\dot{M}_{H_2O}}{\text{Initial wt.}}$		
0.059		0.049-0.072	30	32	1.84	0.0070		
0.060		0.051-0.068	30	32	1.88	0.0071		
0.065	(0.069)	0.052-0.072	29	30	2.17	0.0074		
0.065	(0.069)	0.054-0.072	29	30	2.17	0.0074	0.182	
0.066	(0.070)	0.059-0.070	29	30	2.20	0.0074	0.214	
0.070		0.060-0.076	30	32	2.19	0.0070	0.205	0.781
							0.208	
							0.212	
							0.229	0.831
							0.208	0.784
0.064	(0.066)				2.08(SD ± 0.17)	0.0072	0.199	0.731

egg-laying. Both birds participated, apparently without any qualitative difference. Many scrapes were made before one was used for egg-laying. Some were quickly made or were merely started and not used again; others were persistently revisited and re-excavated. The final nest site was always one of the latter in those instances I was able to follow. Scrape-making was usually preceded by a characteristic posture that I call "V-tilting," in which the bird lowers the foreparts, tilts the hindparts up so that the dorsal surface is at about a 45° angle above horizontal, and often raises the head to a lesser degree (pl. 7). This gives the bird an asymmetrical V-shape in profile and a distinctive stilted posture in which it stalks about rather stiffly; the deep buff color of the posterior underparts is prominently exposed. After the bird assumes this posture, it usually scrapes backward with its feet and then may lower its breast to rest on the substrate and excavate a scrape by pushing backward vigorously with the feet while slowly and sporadically rotating. There may be some pecking and lateral sand-tossing by the bill near the edge of the scrape, but most of the excavating is done with the feet. The hindparts are kept cocked high except in the course of a deep excavation, in which case the bird settles low, slightly abducts the wings, and depresses the tail. In vigorous scraping, sand may be tossed as far as 0.5 m behind the bird. Scrapes may be made with or without the presence of a mate, but usually the mate is nearby. In what appears to be a definite response to Scrape-making, the mate may lower its head even with the back, run up to within 0.3 m of the scraping bird, and then run in a tight half-circle, full circle, or one and a half circles around it. I did not see more than three multiples of a half-circle. During circling the bird may flick the white-tipped tail slightly upward so that it shows above the wing tips. The circling was not consistently followed by any further display-like behavior, but the circling bird often went into a V-tilt and commenced its own Scrape-making. Usually the two birds made scrapes while facing partly or directly away from each other—so often directly away that this seemed to be a definite pattern and not just random chance. The bird which circled the other might later itself be circled while Scrape-making. I could not detect any qualitative difference in the behavior of the two members of a pair, but it is possible that one sex more frequently performed one or the other of these activities.

A pair may make dozens of scrapes before finally settling on a nest site, and a small islet may resemble a miniature battlefield pocked with bomb craters. This extensive Scrape-making by the EP may serve the following functions: continual firming of the pair bond, selection of a generally favorable nesting site, and selection of a particular site in which the texture and moistness of the sand-gravel is suitable for a nest at that time. Either general or specific site conditions, though, may change drastically before the nesting period is over. Also, potential predators are perhaps deprived of firm clues to actual nest location by the numerous scrapes.

I could not identify the final nest site except by the beginning of incubation after laying of the first egg. Even up to the day before egg-laying, I saw members of pairs V-tilting and Scrape-making at many alternative sites. As mentioned previously, false Scrape-making is frequently used as a Distraction Display after egg-laying and after chick-hatching, and scrapes are also made in which chicks are brooded or concealed. The distraction and chick-brooding activities are not usually preceded by the V-tilt posture, although this may be briefly assumed. Pairs that have lost eggs or newly-hatched chicks may commence sporadic V-tilting and Scrape-making within a day or two after the loss, whether or not this leads to a second nesting.

The size of a fully-excavated scrape is about 15 cm in diameter and 5 cm deep, and those finally used for nesting are (initially at least) in dry sand or sand-gravel. The scrape is always in the open and in full sun and never close to a plant that is large enough to provide shade or concealment. No bits of vegetation, shells, pebbles or any materials are ever gathered or placed around the nest, and I never saw an EP pick up or manipulate any such materials except in connection with foraging.

COPULATION

Despite intensive observation of many pairs of EPs during all stages of their reproductive cycle, I saw a total of only seven copulations, four of which were by one pair and one each by three other pairs. The four copulations by the same pair were seen from 11 days to 3 days before egg-laying; of the other three, two copulations were seen in pairs already with eggs but within one or two days after the start of incubation and possibly before the clutch was complete. The last copulation seen was in a pair that had hatched and lost its only chick 5 days earlier. In all cases the copulation was brief, lasting three to five seconds at most, and was not preceded by any specifically precopulatory display or followed by any specifically post-copulatory behavior. In most instances an extremely simple pattern was followed. The members of the pair were active in the usual manner within their territory—Scrape-making, foraging, charging and chasing intruders. Without any apparent stimulus or signal, the female sank slowly (about one second) into a low crouch, ventral surface against the substrate, head lowered even with the back and parallel to it, but neck not extended. The wings and tail were not spread or raised and there was no quivering and no vocalization. The male was always behind the female in her final orientation, and he then ran up from as far as 10 m away and mounted her with no preliminary display or vocalization. During this run the male assumed a posture similar to that often used in the approach to circle a nest-scraping bird. He lowered the head to the same plane as the back and tilted the foreparts down and the hindparts up, so that the entire dorsal surface from head to tail was at an angle of about 45° above horizontal. This posture was not assumed until the female was already crouched. After mounting, the male balanced without spreading or raising his wings and he appeared to achieve a brief cloacal contact by an unhurried lowering and lateral movement of his rectrices that pushed hers up and aside. The movement was not repeated. The female did not raise her head and the male did not lower his to peck at the female's head or to grasp at her bill. After two or three seconds the male dismounted and both birds quickly resumed moving about and foraging. The place of the copulation was never at an existing nest site or beside a site that would be used in the future.

I saw some relatively slight variations on this simple pattern. In a pair that already had two eggs, the male made a half-circle around the crouching female before mounting her, and after dismounting he walked 3 m away, went into a moderate V-tilt posture, and made a few nest-scraping movements. The female had not been nest-scraping, and this was the only instance I saw in which circling was followed by even a putative copulation attempt. In a different pair nine days prior to egg-laying, one of the birds (I could not tell which) during copulation gave three or four cherk notes, not differing from those same notes given in other contexts. In this case the male, after dismounting, did some slight nest-scraping. After another copulation 6 days later, birds of the same pair both preened briefly and gave a quick shake of the ruffled feathers, with the male slightly preceding the female in these activities. In the copulation of the pair that had lost a chick, there were loud clucking sounds from one or both birds.

As copulation in the EP is brief and without obvious preliminaries, it can easily be missed by an observer and it may be more frequent than was apparent to me. Perhaps the simplicity and brevity of copulatory behavior is related to the fact that the strikingly conspicuous plumage pattern of the EP, which is so effective in aggressive behavior, might make the birds exceptionally vulnerable if displayed in a situation in which they were not fully alert and responsive to possible predation.

EGGS

Detailed descriptions and measurements of EP eggs are given in most of the references listed in the Introduction. In general, the ground color is light yellowish-brown and there are numerous small, irregular spots varying in color from reddish-brown to gray. These superficial markings usually appear to be randomly distributed over the entire egg (pls. 8a, b). My measurements of eggs are given in table 1. The usual clutch is two or three eggs, and of those nests in which I examined completed clutches the counts were: one egg: one; two eggs: six; three eggs: seven. The single-egg clutch (table 1, 2) which hatched was in a particularly gravelly sandbar where excavation was difficult and sand was sparse, and these conditions were perhaps limiting in some way. I monitored this nest for 30 days after locating it, and the small dimensions and compactness of the site indicated that it had never contained more than one egg. Koenig (1926) recorded three clutches of four eggs from a total of ten nests in Egypt at about lat. 27°N, and he considered four eggs to be the usual full clutch. I did not find any four-egg clutches at Gambela, which is almost 20° of latitude farther south, and there may be a latitudinal trend in clutch size.

The position of the eggs is variable but generally follows the conventional pattern of small ends directed centrally if there are three eggs. Probably as a result of the contours of the nest scrape, the eggs are often tilted so that their long axes are about 60° above horizontal with the large ends up. I did not find any eggs placed altogether vertically, as reported by Serle (1939). A deep depression excavated in loose sand tends to assume a conical configuration as sand slides to the bottom, and the position of the eggs usually conforms to this configuration.

INCUBATION BEHAVIOR

The incubation behavior of the EP is one of the most interesting and important parts of its life history, and this will be treated in additional detail in the sections on incubation temperatures and egg weight loss. In brief, the eggs are apparently kept completely or almost completely covered with sand during the day whether or not an incubating bird is present. The extent to which the eggs may be uncovered during incubation is difficult to determine because one cannot see under a sitting bird, but when a bird was suddenly flushed from a nest during the day the eggs were almost always found to be completely covered by sand or, infrequently, with at most about 50 mm^2 (per egg) of the upper surfaces exposed. Except in cases of extremely sudden alarm, a departing adult always tosses some sand over the nest site with the bill, whether or not some egg surface is showing. Most eggs that I observed were only shallowly covered to a depth of about 2 mm to 3 mm, but in a few nests the upper surface of the eggs was covered by as much as 5 mm to 10 mm of sand. Brehm (1879) and Koenig (1926) stated that eggs were buried to a depth of 10 cm to 12 cm, but neither specified whether this depth referred to the top or the bottom of the eggs. In any case, I believe the figure must be an error as I do not think it possible for an EP to excavate that deeply in loose sand; the walls of a small-diameter excavation simply collapse and refill it before that depth can be reached. As the maximum egg length is slightly over 3 cm, even a vertically-positioned egg would have had to be covered with at least 7 cm of sand above its uppermost point, which my experience indicates is most unlikely. Possibly a figure of 10 mm to 12 mm (not cm) above the upper surface of the eggs was meant. Only the bill is used to cover the eggs with sand, and the covering is always done by an antero-posterior movement. While the bird stands, it extends the head forward and downward, thrusts the opened bill into the sand, and then quickly draws it posteriorly so that sand is tossed under the bird and on to the nest (pls. 9a-b). The description is ponderous, but the movement is quick and even a few strokes can fully cover the eggs. The covered nest is essentially even with the level of the surrounding sand. If the EP leaves the nest without haste, the covering is thorough and the bird turns and tosses on sand from several different points. The EP never uses its feet to kick sand over the eggs as it leaves the nest. On returning, the bird may remove some of the covering sand by tossing it to either side with the bill as is sometimes done in foraging. An EP never uncovers the nest with an antero-posterior motion of the bill. After settling on the nest, the bird may rotate in the scrape and use its feet to kick sand backward, deepening the scrape and doubtless changing the position and perhaps the extent of covering of the eggs. During this activity the bird sits low and partly abducts the wings and depresses the tail, apparently bracing itself with the carpal joints and rectrices as it excavates with first one foot and then the other.

Koenig (1926) reported that he found a fresh EP egg lying entirely uncovered in a nest scrape, and that one of his helpers also found and collected a single uncovered egg. Koenig believed that the first egg remained unburied until the next egg was laid, after which both and any subsequent eggs were kept covered with sand. Koenig did not report (and presumably did not observe) whether adult birds incubated, shaded, or otherwise attended the first egg. At Gambela I found the first egg before the second was laid only in two nests, and in both cases the first egg was attended and kept buried by the parents just as later ones were. I watched both these pairs daily before finding their first eggs and would surely have seen an uncovered egg or a parent incubating it if the first egg had remained unburied until the next was laid. Ambient temperatures at Gambela were so high that an unattended egg, even if buried, could not remain below lethal temperatures for more than a few minutes during the middle part of the day (figs. 2-4). Possibly the first-laid EP egg is not buried if ambient temperatures are not dangerously high, or perhaps the unburied eggs reported by Koenig had been abandoned.

My observations and temperature recordings indicate that, at night, the eggs are about two-thirds uncovered and are continuously incubated by a parent bird. Nest-sitting on largely or completely covered eggs may continue during the cooler early daylight hours which are about one to two hours after sunrise depending on the cloud cover. There usually follows an increasingly warmer period of about one to two hours

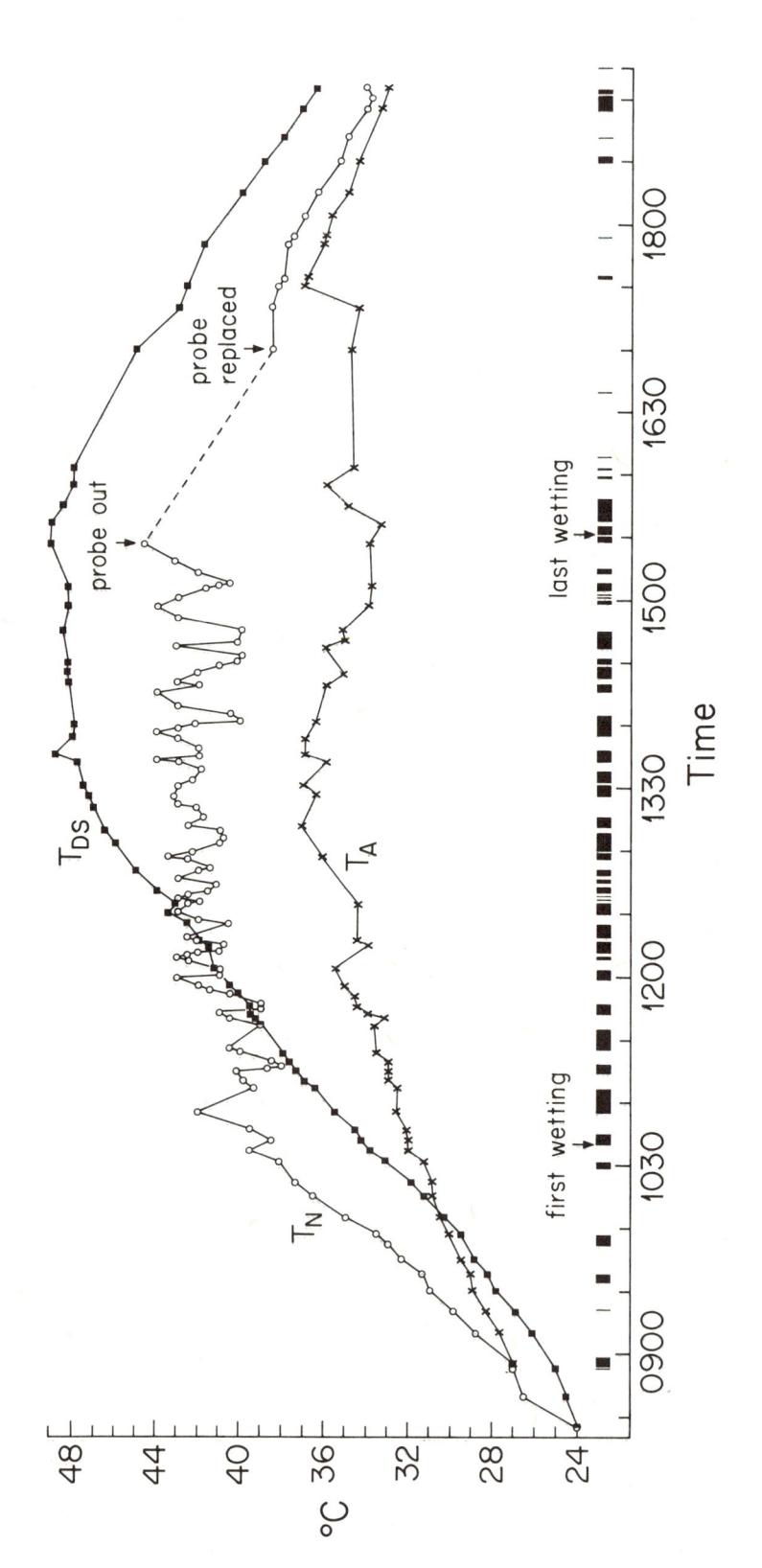

Fig. 2. Ambient and nest temperatures recorded 9 February 1977. T_A = air temperature in shade; T_{DS} = temperature in dry sand near nest, 10 mm below surface; T_N = temperature in nest, 10-15 mm below surface; depth was altered as bird shifted sand. Along the time axis, solid dark marks indicate the duration of attendance at the nest by an adult bird. See table 2 and text for additional details.

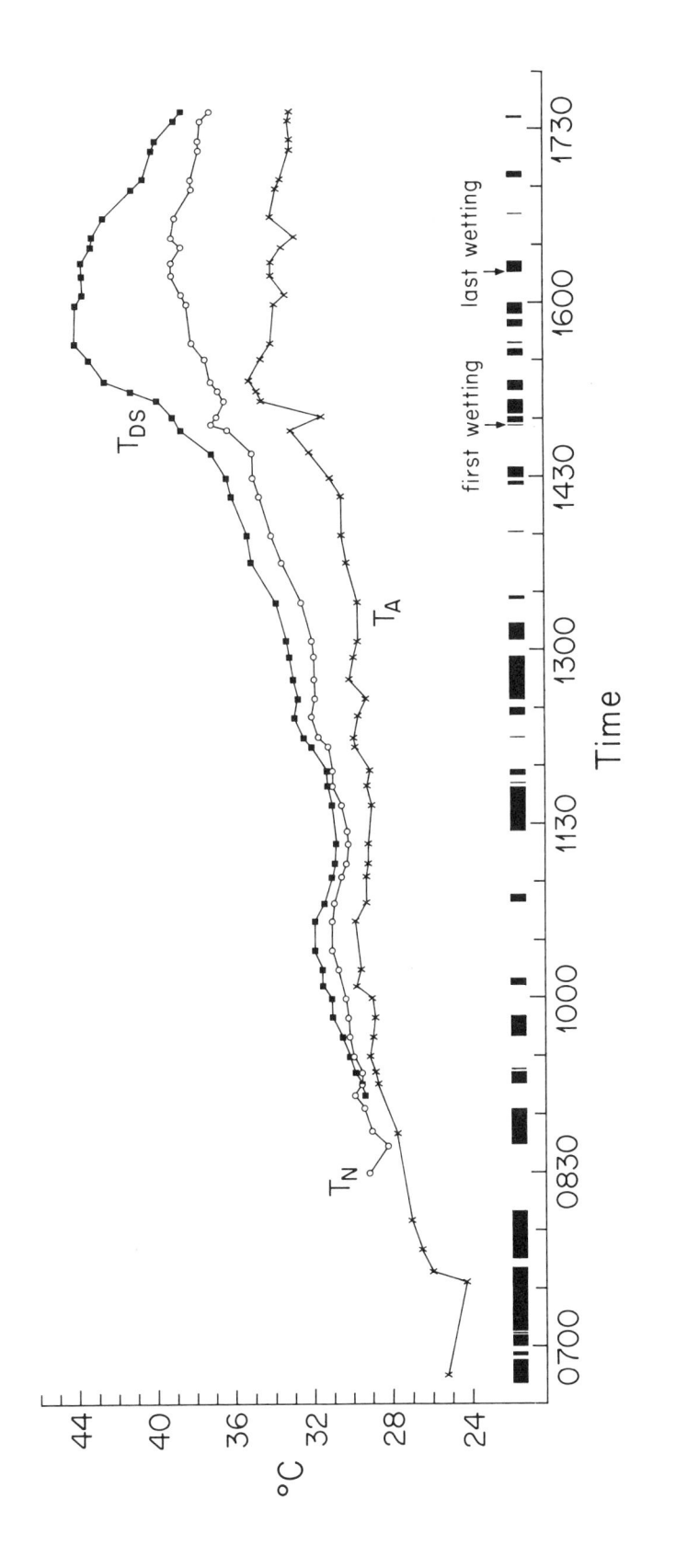

Fig. 3. Ambient and nest temperatures recorded 11 February 1977 at same nest as figure 2. Depth of probe recording T_N and T_{DS}, 20 mm. For definition of symbols and additional details, see figure 1, table 2, and text.

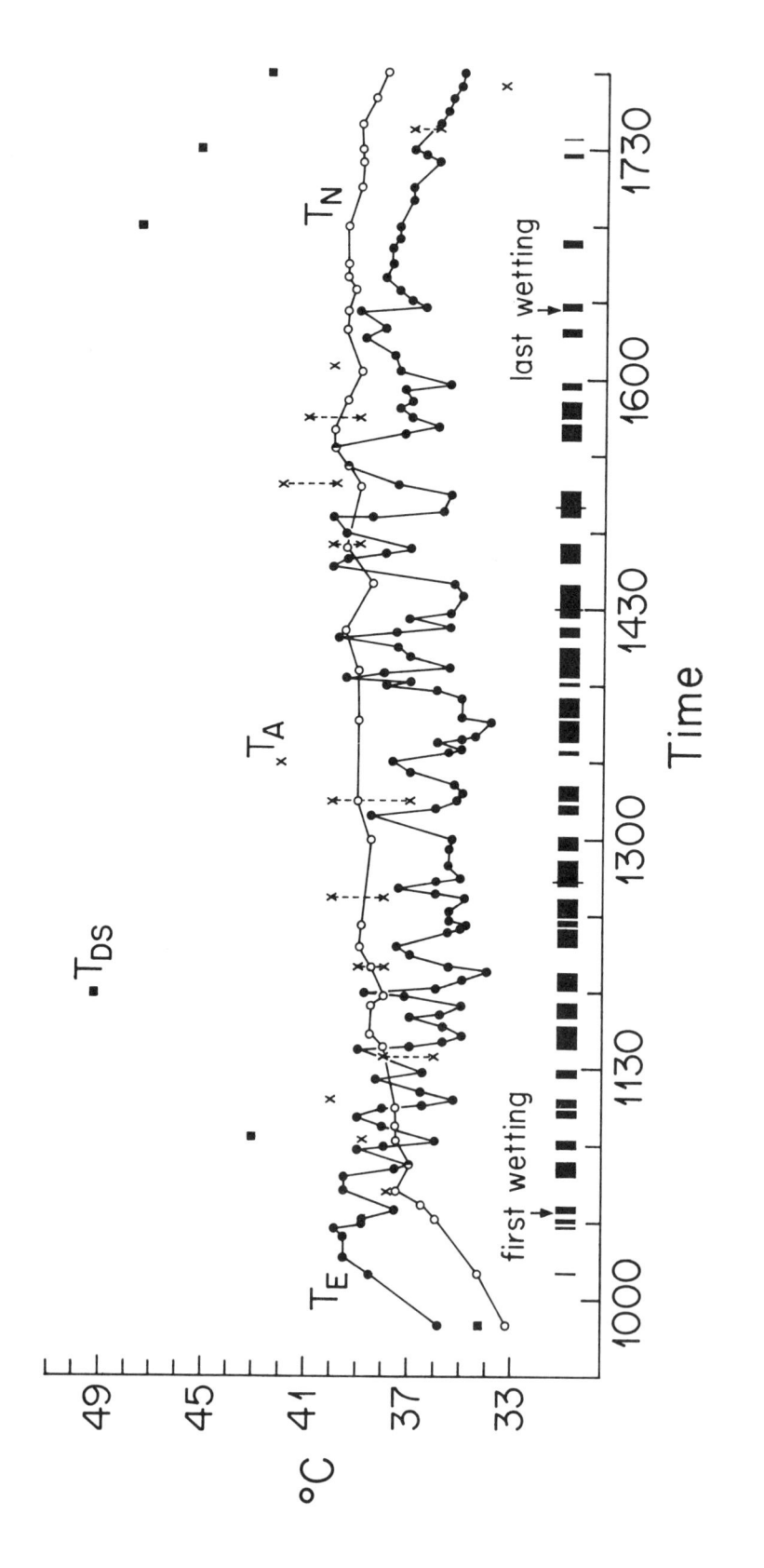

Fig. 4. Ambient, nest and egg temperatures recorded 20 February 1977. T_E = temperature inside egg in nest; other symbols as in figure 2. Depth of probes recording T_N, 15-20 mm; T_{DS}, 20 mm. To avoid clutter, individual points representing T_{DS} and T_A (40 mm above surface) are not joined. Fluctuation in T_A caused by winds is indicated by vertical dashed lines connecting points. Between about 1230 and 1600, T_{DS} exceeded 50°. For additional details, see table 2 and text.

when the covered eggs are largely or completely unattended by the adults, and the temperature in the nest remains within the normal limits for incubation. There is a similar period of little or no parental attendance from about two hours before sunset until as much as one hour after.

During the hottest part of the day, usually from about three to four hours after sunrise to about two or three hours before sunset (a period of six to seven hours), the nest is closely attended by the adult birds. They keep the egg temperature from rising too high by continuously wetting the eggs. Every few minutes the attending adult goes to the river, wades in, soaks its ventral feathers with a stereotyped rocking motion, and returns and settles its wet ventral surface on the nest. This was accurately described by G. Verner (Seebohm, 1888) but not reported by any later observers. Thus, for all of the hottest period of the day, the eggs are completely surrounded by soaking wet sand (pl. 8b). Parents change places at the nest frequently and their behavior is identical. Much of the time an adult bird sits on the covered eggs, leaving only when alarmed or to go to the river for more soaking, or when relieved by its mate. When an adult leaves, it almost always scrapes dry sand over the wet sand around the eggs, effectively concealing the nest. On most days solar radiation is intense and the air and substrate temperatures are extremely hot and EPs follow the behavior pattern just described. On cloudy and cool days, however, the adult birds do not soak their feathers and wet the sand of the nest but attend it continually, sometimes shifting the sand cover with the bill, sometimes sitting on it quietly, sometimes settling low and excavating with the feet. Evidently the parents somehow monitor the nest temperature and adjust their behavior accordingly. Thermoregulation of the eggs is more fully discussed in the section on Incubation Temperatures.

SOAKING

The soaking behavior is highly stereotyped and is performed identically by adult birds of both sexes. It apparently commences in fully expressed form on the first day of egg-laying and not before, and continues with diminished frequency until about the second week after chick-hatching. Soaking enables adult birds to wet eggs or young chicks during the hottest part of the day and thus prevents egg and chick temperatures from reaching dangerously high levels. It must also result in beneficial heat loss by the adults. Soaking behavior declines as chicks become more active and self-sufficient and ceases altogether by the time the chicks are about two weeks old.

To soak, an adult EP wades into quiet, shallow water at the river's edge until its ventral body surface is immersed. The bird then rapidly rocks up and down, alternately lowering and raising its fore- and hindparts in an antero-posterior plane. There are always multiple rockings, usually in bouts of five or six, but sometimes fewer and sometimes up to at least ten or twelve without pause. Often a bird pauses momentarily and then commences another bout of rocking. The bird may remain in one place or continue to move forward as it rocks. While rocking, the head is not lowered in relation to the body, the wings are not spread or drooped, but the unspread tail is sometimes cocked up slightly above the folded wing tips. With the last rock, and only then, the bill is tilted down and momentarily dipped into the water (pl. 10). If this is a drinking action it is extremely brief and little water could be ingested. The behavior pattern as a whole somewhat resembles that of sandgrouse (Pteroclidae), which also thoroughly soak the ventral feathers. The two species (*Pterocles namaqua* and *P. burchelli*) that I have seen soaking may dip the bill several times in the course of the action, not just once at the end.

As the EP emerges from the water its abdominal and posterior breast feathers are dripping wet. Usually the bird needs only a few seconds to walk or run to its nest or buried chick, and the water loss in this interval is negligible. Nevertheless, the bird may sometimes appress the ventral feathers so that the contour of the underside appears smooth, and this may cause retention of a little water that might otherwise be lost. Most nests I have seen are less than 10 m from the water's edge, with the most distant being about 30 m away. On reaching its nest, the bird fully extends the wet ventral feathers and settles on the substrate, often with widely spread legs (pl. 11). The temperature of the river water in the shallows during the hottest part of the day, when the EPs soak, is about 27° to 28°.

To see if the ventral feathers of the EP are modified in a way that facilitates water uptake (as in sandgrouse), I plucked pectoral and abdominal feathers from museum specimens of a male and female EP collected in Sudan in March when they were presumably breeding. I examined these microscopically and also examined ventral feathers from several species of sandpipers and plovers and from a male Yellow-throated Sandgrouse, *Pterocles gutturalis,* a species with modified feathers described and figured by Cade and Maclean (1967). The EPs' ventral feathers closely resemble those of the sandpipers and plovers and show no structural modifications like those of the sandgrouse. In the former group of charadriiforms the ventral feathers have interlocking hooked barbules in the distal medial parts; the barbules become elongate and filamentous proximally and laterally, and there is a well-developed, largely filamentous aftershaft. In the sandgrouse, the tightly coiled barbules around the barbs of the central part of the feather represent a totally different arrangement.

I observed under the microscope the effects of a drop of water placed on ventral feathers of the Western Sandpiper (*Calidris mauri*), Snowy Plover (*Charadrius alexandrinus*), the EP, and the Yellow-throated Sandgrouse. In the latter species the effect was striking; within seconds, the barbules uncoiled as water passed in among them. In all of the former group of species, the feathers were readily wetted but without any change in the orientation of the barbules; water evidently passes in by capillarity without any special movement of feather parts. I conclude that the ventral feathers of the EP are not structurally modified in association with its soaking and nest-wetting behavior. This is not surprising in view of the close proximity of EP nest sites to sources of water.

In change-overs of mates at the nest there is no display, ceremony, or vocalization. Usually the nonattending mate walks by within a few m, the attending bird leaves, and the mate then comes to the nest. Sometimes the nonattending bird comes right up to its mate on the nest before places are changed. More rarely the attending bird does not leave at once and the mate walks about close by without conspicuous agitation until the first bird leaves, usually in less than one minute. Sometimes the approaching mate does some lateral sand-tossing with its bill as it walks around. Although no vocalizations are given just before or during change-overs, a vocalization from either the attending or nonattending bird sometimes seems to signal its presence to the other, but this was not correlated with change-overs in any immediate or consistent way (see Vocalizations).

An incubating EP does not defecate while on the nest or near it, at least not consistently, so there is no accumulated ring of droppings that might reveal the location of the nest site while the parents are away.

The eggs are definitely turned, as shown by changed positions of marked eggs, but apparently not regularly and perhaps only fortuitously in the course of excavating and sand-shifting by the feet. I found some eggs turned through 180° after a twenty-four hour interval, but I do not know if the turning was rapid or gradual. I never saw an EP use its bill to move an egg in any way, but this may possibly happen at night. The eggs do not seem to be turned during the hot hours, while being wetted.

INCUBATION PERIOD

This is defined by Drent (1970) as "the number of days required for development under the conditions prevailing in the nest after the pattern of parental behavior typical of the species has been fully established." In the EP such parental care necessarily starts from the time of laying of the first egg, at least during the daylight hours (pp. 30-31). A clutch of three eggs could not be produced in less than three days, and if incubation commenced with the first egg the expectation would be that they would hatch on successive days. In the two three-egg clutches that I monitored in which all three hatched, the pattern of hatching differed. In one case, two eggs hatched on the first hatching day, one in the morning and the other in the afternoon; the third egg hatched the next morning. In the other case (see below) one egg hatched on the morning of the first day and the other two hatched on the next day, one in the morning and the other in the afternoon. In these two three-egg clutches, however, I had earlier removed the smallest of the three eggs for most of one day while substituting a thermocouple-implanted egg for temperature monitoring (figs. 4, 5). I kept the removed eggs within the range of normal incubation temperature and both hatched apparently normal chicks, but the experiment may have had an effect on the time of hatching.

I do not know if the parents attend the eggs at night before the clutch is complete. If they do not, this would slow down development of the first-laid egg(s) and would work toward more synchronous hatching.

Because of these uncertainties and others described below, I could only ascertain the minimum incubation period even in the most completely monitored nests. In my calculations I assume that the eggs were laid during the day, and probably in the morning. I count the day on which the first egg is laid as the first day of incubation and the day of hatching as the last. For example, if an egg were laid on 2 March (presumably in the morning) and hatched on the morning of 2 April the incubation period would be 31 days.

The incubation period of the EP is at least 28 to 31 days. Because the eggs are usually not visible I was able to infer and check for the presence of the first egg only from the first observation of incubation, and there was no way to determine how much earlier (if at all) the egg might have been laid. I recorded hatching in seven nests, but in only one of these did I feel reasonably sure that I had observed the first day of incubation (two other such "first-day" nests were abandoned before hatching). In this most complete case I observed incubation at 1200 on 2 March, visited the nest at 1800, and found and marked one egg (table 1, 4a). On my next visit, at 1800 on 3 March, I found and marked a second egg (4b); on the next day, same time, there were still only

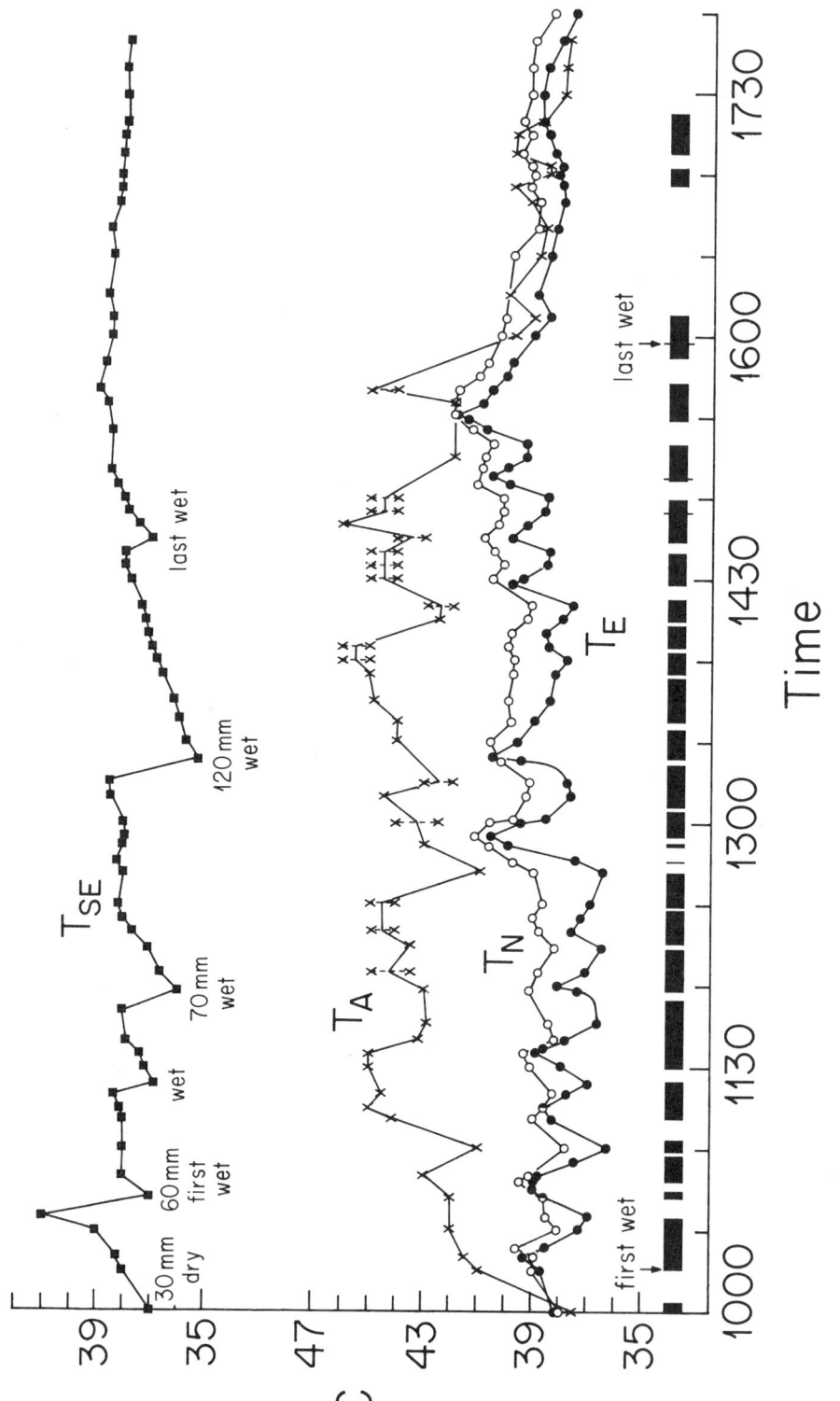

Fig. 5. Ambient, nest, and egg temperatures recorded 19 March 1977. For definitions of symbols, see figures 2 and 4. Vertical line through solid bar symbolizing parental attendance indicates immediate replacement of one bird by the other. Depth of probe recording T_N, 15-20 mm. T_{SE} = temperature of sand around egg which had been removed from nest, buried, and maintained by me within the indicated temperature range by successively deeper burials and wettings. For additional details, see table 2 and text.

two. I foolishly assumed that the clutch was complete at two, but when I next checked the nest on 9 March a third egg (4c) was present. This third egg, which may have been infertile (see Incubation Temperatures), did not hatch. Both the others were newly hatched on the morning of 2 April, giving incubation periods of at least 31 days for the first and 30 days for the second.

In another nest, incubation was first observed on 3 February, but I had not checked the site the previous day. When first visited at 1630 on 5 February it had two eggs, and when next visited on 20 February there were three eggs. One of the first two eggs was newly-hatched on the morning of 5 March; the other of these was newly-hatched the next morning (6 March), and the third (last-laid) egg was hatched by that afternoon. These dates give minimum incubation periods of 30 days for the first egg, 29 for the second, and 28.5 for the third, assuming that the latter was laid on the morning of 6 February.

The only nest with a single egg was discovered when I noted an incubating bird on 21 February, but the site was not regularly checked earlier. This egg (table 1, 2) was newly hatched on 24 March, giving an incubation period of at least 31 days.

A nest in which incubation was first noted on 19 February had a clutch of two and hatched one egg on 21 March, giving an incubation period of at least 30 days if that was the first egg laid. The other egg was cracked a few days before hatching time and had spoiled.

Other monitored nests hatched eggs 20 to 26 days after first observation of incubation, and I had no reason to believe that they were discovered on the first day of laying.

The data above show or suggest that in two of the nests the third egg was not laid until at least a one-day interval after the second. As I could not be absolutely sure that I found the first egg on the day it was laid, it is possible that the first two eggs also were not laid on successive days but only after a one-day interval. For purposes of calculation in subsequent sections I have chosen 30 days as a reasonable approximation of the average incubation period of the EP.

The incubation period is not a time of quiet sitting and reduced energy expenditure for the EP. The incubating bird is perpetually alert, is constantly looking up and around, and is up and off the nest many times as predators or competitors approach. These activities usually involve vigorous sand-shifting with the bill and often an aggressive charge. In addition, the need to wet the eggs requires frequent trips to the river. The decline in body weight of adults during the nesting period (p. 54) may be related to their high level of activity throughout that time.

SECOND CLUTCHES

Circumstantial evidence strongly suggests that, in two instances, pairs that lost eggs relatively early in the breeding season laid second clutches and successfully hatched them. In the first case a clutch of two eggs was destroyed by a predator, probably a Pied Crow, on 23 or 24 February. Another clutch of two eggs (table 1, 3a-b) was laid only about 2 m or 3 m from the first site, and as these were pipped on 5 April they must have been laid around 5 March, about 10 days after the first loss. In the second case I collected two eggs (table 1, 6a-b; possibly not a full clutch) from a nest on 13 February, and a clutch of three eggs (table 1, 1a-c) was subsequently laid within about 10 m of the first nest. These eggs hatched on 29 and 30 March, so the date of laying must have been around 28 February, about 15 days after I took the first eggs.

In view of the apparently long pre-egg stage, the 30 day incubation period, and a period of at least four weeks for post-hatching parental care, I doubt that any pairs of EPs that raise young to self-sufficiency attempt a second nesting in the same season. If the earliest-nesting pair that I observed had laid a second clutch of eggs after their young were about five weeks old, the laying date would have been about 12 March and the hatching date would have been at least a week later than that of any other clutches known to me but still many weeks before the end of the dry season. Second broods thus seem possible in terms of time available, but doubtful in view of the prolonged high level of energy expenditure required for successful nesting.

PIPPING

Pipping is first detectable as a tiny, radiating fracture toward the large end of the egg, and it may be at any point of the circumference and not necessarily at the surface which is uppermost at the time. This is followed by the flaking off of a chip of shell about 1 mm wide, which reveals the contrasting white shell membrane. Next, the shell membrane is punctured and the shell fracture enlarged so that the tip of the bill with the egg tooth is visible. I did not find multiple pips all around the egg, and further cracking of the shell progressed from the original opening and nearby points. I did not hear any vocalizations from unhatched chicks, but I examined eggs at this stage only for a few minutes so as not to risk harmful disturbance of the hatching process. In most cases eggs found pipped early in the day and still only pipped by late afternoon were hatched by the next morning, but in one case such a pipped egg did not hatch until midafternoon the next day, and in another case a pipped egg with the shell membrane still intact at 0900 hatched fully by 1400. Those found hatched by morning may possibly have hatched during the night.

HATCHING

I observed the hatching process through to completion in two nests, and in four other nests I found newly hatched chicks present on my first visit of the morning. Hatching apparently proceeds as in other charadriiform birds despite the fact that the pipped egg is largely or completely buried in the sand, and the sand is usually thoroughly wet for many hours. A parent bird was on the nest during most of the two hatchings that I monitored, so it was impossible to observe the hatching process close-up and continuously. At one of these nests, an egg that was only slightly pipped at 0900 was fully hatched five hours later and the chick had emerged from under the sand. I watched during this entire interval and I feel certain that the hatching egg was never more than slightly exposed, if at all. In another nest, I examined two slightly pipped but unhatched eggs at 1015 and found them completely under wet sand and covered with a surface layer of dry sand. The parents were continually attending and wetting the eggs from then until 1155, when I again examined the nest. One egg was more fully pipped with the chick's egg tooth showing; the other egg showed no progress, but the uppermost one-third of both was now uncovered. The parents continued to sit-soak-sit, and at 1400 I again went to the nest. The more advanced egg was partly hatched, with only the chick's head showing above the sand (pl. 12). I removed more sand and found that the chick's body was about half out of the shell. I then covered the chick with sand up to its head. By 1510, when next examined after continual parental attendance, the chick was fully hatched, crouched flat, and lightly covered with sand so that only its contours and some wisps of down showed. The other egg was still only slightly pipped and was lying horizontally with the upper half exposed; the pip, however, was under the sand. At 1700 the hatched chick was fully above the sand in the nest, its down dry. Pipping was proceeding in the other egg under the sand and it had hatched fully by the following morning.

I did not see any removal of hatched eggshells by the parent birds, but in one case I found large pieces of shell 1.5 m from the nest on the day of hatching of the last of three chicks. In other nests, it appeared that the empty shells from first hatchings were ground into small fragments by shifting about of the sand-gravel by the parent birds' feet in the course of continued incubating and brooding. The white inner surface of the hatched eggshell would be highly conspicuous at most nest sites, and removal or pulverization of such shells is doubtless advantageous.

ROLES OF THE PARENTS DURING HATCHING

I could detect no qualitative differences in the behavior of the members of a pair at this time. If a chick is hatching or has recently hatched in about the first five hours after sunrise (largely before the most intense heat of the day), only one parent seems to attend the nest for relatively long spans lasting at least one to perhaps several hours. Its mate often forages nearby, and if there is a change-over during this time, the bird that relieves usually has a long span of attendance also.

As the ambient temperature rises and nest-soaking behavior commences, the parents quickly shorten the intervals between change-overs and may relieve each other every few minutes. Usually a bird makes several trips to the river for soaking during its attentive span, but sometimes the members of the pair alternate at the nest, with each one soaking before its return. During the hot hours the nest is kept wet as long as it contains eggs or chicks or both.

ACTIVITY OF NEWLY-HATCHED CHICKS

Newly-hatched chicks were first described by Butler (1931). In general, the back and the top of the head are light grayish-brown finely speckled with black. Otherwise, chicks have a head pattern similar to that of adults—white superciliary stripes that meet posteriorly to form a white nuchal patch, and black stripes through the eye that meet on the nape below the white area. The underparts are white and there is no trace of a pectoral band. The downy wings are also white (pl. 13). There is a white egg tooth on the tip of the upper mandible only, and the mouth lining is dark red. The legs and feet are blue-gray, as in adults. The first set of contour feathers has essentially the same pattern and color as that of adults, but with some brownish tips that later wear away.

Chicks of the EP are precocial, category 3, according to the criteria of Nice (1962). At the time of hatching, a chick is well covered with down, the eyes are fully open, and within less than an hour it is capable of rapid running and feeds itself when food is brought (see below), although it does not forage independently. The chick leaves the nest at some time during the day of hatching, often for only short sorties and returns, but has left permanently by the end of that day. A chick may remain in the nest for most of the first day, or it may make its first sortie within an hour or two of hatching. If more than one chick is in the nest, there is more likely to be early activity by the most recently hatched. In some nests in which a chick had hatched before my first morning visit, I found the chick completely covered with sand, or so nearly covered that only traces of down were visible. In the former situation, I discovered the chick only by probing into the sand and then clearing it away. In another case, recently-hatched chicks with their down not yet dry were in the open and out of the nest but only about 0.2 m away from it. I returned these chicks to the nest site (which still contained an egg) in midmorning for photographic purposes, and they remained there for about five hours and were continually attended by the parents. In still another nest, each of two morning-hatched chicks on successive days had moved from 6 m to 17 m away from the nest by two hours after sunrise.

After most of its early sorties a chick soon came back to the nest if an adult was still there, or returned when a departed adult returned. Adults returned to the nest provided that there was still an egg or another chick in it; otherwise, an adult would go to a chick in its new location and brood it, or would quickly make a scrape close by to which the chick would readily come. Recently-hatched chicks also may excavate the sand around themselves with their feet. In the case of the nest in which the chicks had moved many meters away shortly after hatching, I had the impression that the adults were leading each chick away from the nest site by making repeated scrapes ahead of the chicks in a given direction. This took the chicks from a highly exposed site 30 m from the water's edge to a sparsely vegetated part of the sandbar that provided some cover and was close to the water. In all cases, both parents closely monitored the activity of the chicks, when necessary brooding them, or cooling them by wetting, or concealing them by covering with sand (see below).

I could not see any nocturnal adult-chick interactions, but I presume that chicks are brooded by the parents during the night. I presume this in view of the close parental attentiveness throughout the day and the probability that unbrooded, recently-hatched chicks could not thermoregulate effectively at the usual nocturnal ambient temperatures that fall as low as 20°C.

Chicks may show aggression toward siblings as early as the day of hatching and continue this to an age of at least three weeks. In the nest in which a chick hatched between 0900 and 1400, the newly-hatched chick was repeatedly and vigorously pecked by its earlier-hatched sibling that was still in the nest. I could see no obvious reason for the attacks in terms of competition for space or position or food. The older chick persistently pecked at the white spot on the nape of the younger one, and the latter did not move away but seemed uninjured by the blows. Among older siblings that forage for themselves and with the parents (see below), one chick or juvenile may run at another and chase it away from a good foraging spot or away from a foraging adult.

Feeding.

As is typical of coursers, by the latter part of the day of hatching the parents bring food to the chicks either in the nest or away from it if they have moved. The food is small insects or other arthropods visibly carried by the adult in its bill. A chick does not beg or solicit feeding in any way, nor does it reach up to the adult's bill. The parent bird lowers its head and puts the food down in front of the chick, which quickly seizes and swallows it. I could not be certain if the adult always releases the food before the chick's peck, but the food is taken at ground level at the tip of the adult's bill. Feedings are not frequent, but there may be several during the latter part of the day of hatching. I did not see chicks forage by themselves on the day of hatching or on several subsequent days, and I saw the parents continue to bring food occasionally for many more days. Sometimes food is obtained hundreds of meters away on the mainland and carried in flight. The total amount of food brought must be very small, and most of a chick's food is obtained by accompanying a foraging adult. The parent birds forage in the ways previously described, and a chick accompanies one or the other and picks up prey exposed near the tip of the adult's bill. This is particularly noticeable during stone-turning, which the chick is too small to do; the adult exposes the food and waits as the chick pecks at it. Sometimes a chick wanders away from a nonforaging adult, but runs to it (without any vocal signal) as it commences foraging again. Often one or more chicks run back and forth between their two foraging parents.

Drinking.

Chicks may go to the river and drink as early as the day of hatching (pl. 13). While still in the nest, however, chicks may take water from the wet ventral feathers of a brooding parent. This is not done regularly or frequently and is difficult to see, but after first seeing what appeared to be drinking from the feathers, I watched for it with extreme care at several nests. I clearly saw that occasionally a chick raised its head, pecked at the dripping tip of a wet feather cluster, and swallowed. It is possible that the chick was pecking at adhering sand grains or simply at a dangling object, but some water was surely ingested. I doubt that this activity provides an important source of water considering that such drinking is infrequent and that chicks may drink from the nearby river shortly after leaving the nest. The behavior is of interest, however, as it is similar to the much more highly developed pattern of sandgrouse, the males of which carry water in their soaked belly-feathers for considerable distances to their chicks (Cade and Maclean, 1967). In the EP the drinking by chicks from soaked feathers seems to be only an incidental consequence of nest-wetting by adults, but it suggests a possible early step in the evolution of the highly derived behavior of sandgrouse.

Bathing.

Chicks may bathe at the river's edge as early as the day of hatching and the bathing motions are similar to those of adults. Thus, although chicks are often exposed to high ambient temperatures and intense solar radiation, their potential thermoregulatory problems are greatly reduced by their ready access to water. Water lost through evaporative cooling (panting) can easily be replaced by drinking, and heat can be lost by wetting the body surface. The water temperature in the shallows at the edge of the river does not rise above about 27° to 28°, which is far lower than air and substrate temperatures during most of the day.

Nest sanitation.

While still in the nest, chicks sometimes voided feces that were small, dark-colored, and pasty, and I saw such droppings carried away in the bill by an adult bird. I did not see any gelatinous fecal sacs or any liquid droppings produced by chicks in the nest.

COVERING OF YOUNG BIRDS WITH SAND

Butler (1931) first described covering of downy chicks by adults in case of danger, although Percival (1906) earlier reported that "from... under about a quarter-of-an-inch of sand I drew a three-parts-grown Egyptian Plover!" The EP appears to be unique among all birds in that it not only covers newly-hatched chicks still in the nest but also covers them after they have left the nest up to an age at which they have well-developed contour feathers and are more properly called juveniles. I observed and photographed chick-covering many times among many different EP families (pls. 14a-c, 15a-b). In the first few post-hatching days chicks are routinely covered with sand by adults whenever danger seems to threaten, which is usually many times each day. As the young birds grow larger the practice becomes less frequent and the largest juveniles of known age that I saw covered were 22 or 23 days old. Under similar circumstances 6 days later, I did not see these same juveniles covered although they still did not fly at that age.

Chicks are covered with sand by adults with exactly the same antero-posterior movement of the bill used in covering eggs (pl. 9a-b). A newly-hatched chick still in the nest is covered with sand along with any unhatched eggs whenever the attending parent leaves. On the day of hatching a chick that is only a few cm from a brooding adult on the nest may return there and be covered, but if farther away it will probably be covered in situ. The stimulus that prompts chick-covering is the approach of any potential predator. This is usually a fairly fast-moving, low-soaring kite or Pied Crow, in which case the covering may be hasty and incomplete, but if the potential predator approaches slowly and is detected at a distance, the covering of the chicks is usually so thorough that the contours are completely invisible under the sand. I found it difficult or impossible to locate such fully-buried chicks unless I was able to watch the covering through binoculars and fix the exact location. Both parents participate equally in covering chicks. Each parent works with a different chick, not together on the same one, and the activity appears frantic when two or three chicks are widely separated. Usually they are not together and are covered separately; only once did I find two chicks covered over together, and they were in side-to-side contact and oriented head-to-tail (pls. 14a-c). A third chick of this brood was not with these two but was also buried.

When an adult approaches a chick for covering, the chick crouches as flat as possible with the head lowered and approximately even with the back. It usually crouches in a slight depression in the sand, and as such depressions are nearly everywhere the chick need not move more than a few steps, if at all, to find one. Larger young birds such as those about 21 days old may excavate a depression with their feet, in the manner of adults. I did not hear any vocalization from chicks or any vocal signal by adults that was closely or specifically associated with crouching and covering. Chicks might cease moving and crouch, however, on hearing loud, aggressive calls from adults even though this was not necessary followed by chick-covering—as when the cause of the calls was an intruding EP. During covering, sand is tossed over the chick from any or all directions, after which the adult leaves. When temperatures are high and danger is still present but not too close, adults soak their ventral feathers and come to wet the buried chicks.

Butler (1931) wrote: "I saw one of these Plovers drink at the water's edge, run up onto a sandbank, stop and regurgitate the water, and then settle down over the spot to brood." He then found a small chick completely buried at that spot. This account has been widely quoted and has also been used as the basis for an illustration (Cameron, in Perrins, 1976). I saw many instances of buried chicks being wetted by the ventral feathers but never by recognizable regurgitation. I cannot help but wonder if Butler saw the terminal bill-dip (pl. 10) of a soaking adult bird and then saw it test the sand at the nest with its bill (p. 47). He may have interpreted this as drinking and regurgitation, and indeed it may be, but if so the amount of water provided must be very small compared to that carried in the soaked ventral feathers. I remain puzzled that Butler never reported soaking by the EP, as I found it to be invariable and frequent among all the nesting pairs that I observed.

When danger is no longer present, adults may come and start to dig out the chick with lateral sand-tossing by the bill, at which time the chick raises itself as well and is quickly uncovered. Chicks are not buried any more deeply than needed for full concealment and they have no difficulty in raising themselves out of the sand. If not soon visited by an adult, a buried chick may raise its head above surface and then emerge fully if the activity of adults does not indicate persistent danger. I do not know how long a chick may remain fully covered, but I think not more than a few minutes at most and probably usually not that long without at least raising the bill and part of the head just out of the sand.

A remarkable aspect of the behavior of covered chicks is their almost complete immobility when discovered and touched or even when taken out and gently handled. This is so even if the bird is only partly and lightly covered and even in three-week-old juveniles except when the latter are more than slightly handled (pl. 15a-b). Many times, I exposed a downy chick by clearing away the sand with my fingers, picked up the chick, and then replaced it and covered it with sand. During all this the chick never vocalized and either did not move or did so just enough to maintain its low-crouched posture. The eyes, however, were usually wide open and conspicuous. Most such young chicks remained inert even if turned over while being held in the hand, but rarely one would struggle to get away. One approximately three-week-old juvenile remained tensely immobile when uncovered and first removed, but when further manipulated it suddenly leaped away and ran off for a long distance at high speed. Another of about the same age suddenly jumped out of its hollow and ran off while I was removing sand slowly and in stages for photographic purposes.

In one EP family I saw chick-covering continue persistently as though programmed, even though it seemed detrimental to the chick. This took place after hatching of the only single-egg clutch that I found, at a site on a small, low island on which there was relatively little sand and much gravel. At the time of hatching there had been an unseasonal rise in the level of the river which reduced the area of the island and caused wetting by capillarity of all the exposed sand. The reduced area of the island concentrated visiting wading birds and raptors around the vicinity of the EP nest, and the EPs responded by frequent attempts to cover the chick. Not only was sand sparse but it was also wet, so that for most of the first post-hatching day the chick was kept almost constantly damp. It felt chilled to my touch, but the parents did not refrain from throwing more wet sand over it when approached nor did the chick take any counter-action. It appeared to me that the uncovered chick, when crouched and immobile, was extremely inconspicuous and that the covering activity of the parents added no significant concealment and only called attention to the chick's location. I doubted that the chick could long survive under these conditions, but there was no test of this as the river continued to rise and before full submergence of the island the chick had disappeared and the parent birds were no longer present.

INCUBATION TEMPERATURES

One of the most interesting questions concerning the reproductive biology of the EP has been whether the buried eggs are unattended for most of the day and thus incubated largely by solar heat, or whether the adults must frequently attend the nest and control the egg temperatures by covering or uncovering the eggs and by shading or wetting them. The EP's habit of burying its eggs and wetting them has been known since the nineteenth century and has prompted much speculation about thermoregulation, but not one published account to date includes any actual measurements of temperature within the nest. A related question has been whether or not the EP uncovers and incubates its eggs at night and, if so, to what extent. There are no published observations on nocturnal nest care by the EP.

In previous sections I have described the frequent attendance of both parents individually at the nest and the wetting of the buried eggs during the hottest part of the day. I also recorded temperature data which provide a basis for fuller interpretation of the birds' behavior. To measure temperatures within and without nests, I used a Yellow Springs Instrument Company battery-operated multichannel-thermistor thermometer with a variety of sensor probes. To measure temperatures within eggs, I used a copper-constantan thermocouple and an S-B Systems battery-operated thermocouple thermometer. I used fine-gauge copper and constantan wire to make thermocouples which were inserted in eggs; I then soldered the free ends to long lengths of heavier-gauge copper and constantan wire for connection to the thermometer at a suitable distance from the nest. I soldered thermocouple wire connections in the field when necessary with a battery-operated Wahl Iso-Tip soldering iron. To place the thermocouple inside an egg I made a hole with a needle in the large end (so as to enter the air cell first and minimize leakage of albumin), inserted the thermocouple to the desired extent and position, and sealed the opening with a quick-drying cement of the type used in construction of model airplanes. The cement formed a leak-proof seal and firmly fixed the wires in place.

I placed a thermocouple-egg in an EP nest as a substitute for one of the birds' own eggs, or as an addition in the case of the one-egg clutch. I kept the temperature around each removed egg between 35° and 39°, except for brief periods when it went slightly above or below those limits. At the end of a period of temperature monitoring, the birds' own egg was returned to the nest in place of the thermocouple-egg, and the position and orientation of the latter was carefully checked. I found no indication that the birds made any distinction between the thermocouple egg and their own, and as buried eggs are not regularly turned during the day the position and orientation usually remained the same for the duration of the experiment. I monitored thermocouple-egg temperatures in the manner described above in five different nests, and in each of these all of the birds' own eggs hatched with two understandable exceptions. In one case, one egg of a clutch of two was later found cracked and the contents decomposed;

the other egg hatched. In the second case, the last-laid egg of a clutch of three was replaced by a thermocouple-egg for nocturnal monitoring. The removed egg (table 1, 4c) was buried in the sand outside the nest at the same depth as those remaining in the nest, and its temperature was allowed to fall with that of the surrounding sand (fig. 6). This egg did not hatch although the other two that remained in the nest did. All other temporarily removed eggs hatched and the chicks from these eggs appeared to be completely normal. In view of this high degree of hatching success, I believe that the monitoring procedures did not adversely affect the normal course of incubation and that the temperatures recorded within the thermocouple-eggs were representative of those within the other eggs in the nest.

Data on ambient temperatures, nest and egg temperatures, and parental attendance during my nest monitorings are given in table 2 and figures 2-6. In addition to the data given in the table and figures, relevant points are: The data of 6, 9, and 11 February are from the same nest (table 2, figs. 2, 3). I think that in this nest the first egg was laid and incubation commenced on 3 February, but an earlier date is possible. These eggs disappeared on 14 February.

The hottest part of the day is usually between 1030 and 1600, extending to 1700 if there are clear skies throughout. Even on clear days, there is often enough water-vapor haze from the river or smoke from grass fires to diminish the power of the sun after about 1600. Temperatures and attentive behavior during the hot period are emphasized as it is the time of maximum danger of heat damage to unattended eggs.

The term (on-off) in table 2 refers to a period of attendance by either mate at the nest (on) and then an absence (off); the return to the nest begins the next (on) period. T_A refers to shaded air temperatures near ground level. T_A's for 5 to 11 February are probably lower than they would have been at the nest site as they were taken at observation sites among rocks or small clumps of grasses and not over open sand. All others were taken at 2 cm to 3 cm above open sand, and should be close to those prevailing at the nest site. T_N refers to temperature of the sand within the nest, recorded by a thermistor probe tip 15 mm to 20 mm below the sand surface at about the level of the lower one-third of the buried eggs. T_E refers to temperatures recorded by a thermocouple within an egg placed in the nest at the same level as the others. In the recordings of 20 and 25 February, the thermocouple junction was positioned in the egg near the inner surface of the shell, approximating the position of the developing embryo in the early stages of incubation. On opening the egg after completing the recordings, I found the junction to be about 7 mm below the upper surface of the egg (as positioned in the nest), about 3 mm medial to the left side, and about 10 mm in from the large end (about one-third of the total egg length, near the point of greatest diameter). The junction thus would have been slightly lateral to the center of a hypothetical early embryo. In the thermocouple-egg used on 13, 14, and 19 March, the junction was positioned in the approximate center of the egg at the point of greatest diameter and was found to be in that place when the egg was later opened.

On-offs were most frequent during the period from 1030 to 1600, when their number approximated thirty on sunny days. On the cloudy 11 February the on-offs were reduced by about one-third. During the hot hours the average duration on was usually slightly less than the average duration off, but the figures were reversed for 19 March during an extremely hot day at a nest at an advanced stage of incubation. A long off period during 1030 to 1600 on a hot day was usually the result of disturbance by

TABLE 2—Attentive Periods (min) and

Date	Duration of Monitoring	Total of on-offs	Range of time intervals on nest; $\bar{X}$ interval	Range of time intervals off nest; $\bar{X}$ interval	On-offs, 1030-1600	Range of time intervals on nest; $\bar{X}$; 1030-1600
5 Feb	1040-1600	32	<1-11; 4.7	<1-14; 5.2	same	same
6 Feb*	0910-1610	32	<1-22; 3.7	<1-44; 7.8	28	<1-22; 4.1
9 Feb*	0820-1905	45	<1-12; 4.3	<1-54; 9.9	31	<1-12; 5.0
11 Feb*	0640-1740	34	1-33; 7.0	<1-39; 12.0	20	1-23; 5.65
20 Feb	0950-1800	39	<1-12; 4.6	<1-32; 6.6	32	1-12; 5.1
25 Feb	1200-1730	22	1-13; 6.0	<1-41; 8.2	—	—
19 March	1000-1800	31	1-25; 9.3	<1-48; 5.0	26	1-25; 9.5

*Same nest

Summary of Temperature Data (°C) at Nests

Range of time intervals off nest; $\bar{X}$; 1030-1600	Weather conditions; T_A	Range of T_N (top line) and T_E (second line), total time	Range of T_N (top line) and T_E (second line), 1030-1600	No. of eggs	Estimated days of incubation	Fig. No.
same	mostly sunny 34.5-40.2	38.0-43.5 —	same —	2	14	—
<1-22; 5.6	full sun 32.0-41.0	unrecorded	unrecorded	3	3?	—
<1-14; 5.3	full sun 27.0-37.2	24.0-44.0 —	38.0-44.0 —	3	6?	2
<1-34; 10.8	cloudy to 1445 24.3-35.0	28.2-39.0 —	31.0-38.2 —	3	8?	3
<1-20; 5.1	full sun to 1700 33.6-42.0	33.0-40.0 34.0-40.0	36.0-40.0 34.0-40.0	3	17	4
—	pale sun 35.7-43.0	38.2-41.0 35.3-41.0	—	2	6	—
1-9.5; 3.3	full sun 35.5-46.0	38.0-42.0 36.3-41.9	38.4-42.0 36.3-41.9	3	20	5

people coming to the island to fish near the nest site, and briefer absences were often caused by approaches to the nest by kites or crows. Even without such disturbances, the attending bird often left the nest to soak or forage or both after no more than about ten minutes of sitting.

On all of the hot days, the adults commence soaking themselves and wetting the buried eggs at about 1030 and continue to do this before every return to the nest throughout the hot period. A relieving mate soaks before coming to the nest, and if the mate does not soon come to relieve, the incubating bird quickly runs to the river, soaks, and returns. The soaking and wetting is closely associated with ambient or nest temperatures or both, however, and is not a programmed activity that proceeds irrespective of environmental conditions. This was clearly shown by the pair whose activities were monitored on 6, 9 (fig. 2), and 11 February (fig. 3). The first two days were hot and the first wettings were noted at 1027 and 1040, respectively, and continued from then on. On 11 February the sun was behind clouds until about 1445 and was fully out from then on. T_N from 0910 and 1445 varied between 29.8° and 34.9°, and neither bird soaked and wetted during this interval; instead, there were relatively long on-off periods. From 1445 to 1457 T_N rose to 37.0°, and at 1457 an adult soaked and wetted the nest for the first time that day. Wettings continued until 1622, by which time ambient temperatures had begun to decline slightly from afternoon highs. At the first nest visit after 1622, the bird appeared to be dry and there were no subsequent wettings. The cooling effect of the wettings is demonstrated by the contrast between nest temperature and that recorded 20 mm down in unshaded dry sand nearby (not given in table 2 but in fig. 3). The latter temperature rose from 37.0° to 44.0° between 1445 to 1540, and began to decline slightly only after 1600.

The effect of over-wetting of the eggs on incubation behavior was shown at a nest that was placed too close to the water's edge. Egg-laying in this nest commenced relatively late, on about 14 March, and a clutch of two was laid. On 17 March I removed one egg for experimental purposes and the birds continued to attend the nest with the single remaining egg. The nest site was originally several m from the river, but an unseasonal rise brought the water's edge to about 1 m from the site and all the sand around and including the nest was wetted by capillarity by 27 March. On the morning of that day I went to the nest site and found the egg almost fully exposed in the wet sand in a shallow excavation about 0.2 m in diameter. The sand was full of bill marks but no EP was in sight and I assumed that the nest was deserted. When I returned at about 1130, during the hottest part of the day, I found the sand around the egg further excavated and the egg still above the surface with patches of wet sand sticking to it. When I withdrew, an EP came and sat low and tightly on the egg. I returned at 1330, and at my approach the sitting bird rose and tried vigorously but unsuccessfully to toss the wet sand over the egg. I did not disturb the bird any further, but when I returned on 30 March the water level had risen above the nest site and I could not find the egg. From these observations I conclude that the response to too much wetness and consequent coolness is to uncover the egg and incubate even though the sun is hot and T_A is high. Also, the approach of danger still brings on the cover-with-sand response even though the sand is damp, cool, and not easily tossed with the bill.

EPs are seldom quiet sitters compared to other ground nesting birds, probably in part because they are conspicuous rather than cryptic and in part because of the need for thermoregulation of the eggs. As the eggs are largely or completely buried, the sitting EP may not receive the kind of thermal-tactile stimulus from them that seems to promote quiet sitting in other birds. Except during extremes of ambient temperature, an adult bird coming to the nest usually pokes its bill into the sand covering the eggs many times before settling and often rises again and does more bill-work, perhaps repeating this several times. Some of the bill-work consists of lateral sand-tossing which removes some sand from around the eggs, and this may be alternated with antero-posterior covering movements. Another use of the bill does not uncover or cover, but involves thrusting the slightly opened bill into the sand around the eggs, then closing and withdrawing it—in short, taking a small beakful of sand from below the surface, then dropping it as the bill is withdrawn and repeating the process several times. I interpret this as testing either the temperature or the humidity of the sand or both, as is evidently done by the Mallee Fowl (*Leipoa ocellata*) in the course of regulating the temperature around its buried eggs (Frith, 1962). This sand-testing is usually the first bill-work done by an EP returning to the nest. Possibly the quick bill-dip (and drink?) that occurs at the end of the soaking ritual cools the tongue and inner surface of the bill and enhances the sensitivity of these structures to high temperatures of the sand around the eggs. After further bill-work (if any) and settling, the bird may excavate sand with the feet as it turns on the nest, presumably changing the position or exposure of the eggs. Foot-excavating is usually done during the cooler periods of the day when the nest is not being regularly wetted. During extreme heat stress, the attending bird usually runs to the river to soak, runs back, and settles on the nest in haste with little or no sand-testing or other bill-work. Presumably the intensity of the heat is so great that there would be little or no advantage to testing temperature at such times. Change-overs at the nest are not only much more frequent during the hot hours, but the birds more readily return to the nest despite the proximity of potential predators or people. As suggested in an earlier section, the frequent Looking-up into the sun may serve to check the sun's position as well as to detect aerial predators. All of the evidence indicates that the adult birds are acutely sensitive to ambient temperatures, monitor them frequently, and act in ways that provide protection for the eggs.

The pattern and effect of nest attentiveness may be seen in detail in figures 4 and 5. Figure 5 documents a day with a clear sky and full sun from sunrise to about 1700, when haze began to obscure it. There was light wind, 2 to 6 mph, for most of the morning, increasing to about 10 mph after 1200 with gusts of 15 mph but becoming intermittent by midafternoon. The varying T_A reflects effects of the winds. T_{DS} designates temperature from a thermistor probe 20 mm down in unshaded dry sand at approximately the same level as the probe in the nest that recorded T_N. From the start of recording, all temperatures ascended at similar rates until 1030, when the first wetting of the eggs diminished T_E. The other temperatures continued to rise, especially T_{DS} which went above 50° and off the scale of the instrument at about 1210 and remained at the above-50° level until at least 1600. T_E was reduced from 39.6° at 1028 to 37.5° at 1035 (by three wettings), and until 1630 it continued to fluctuate up and down according to the absence or presence, respectively, of an attending adult. Each absence exposed the nest to full, hot sun, causing a rapid rise in T_E, and each return brought a wetting and an equally rapid drop in T_E. The probe tip measuring T_N was at a deeper level than that within the egg recording T_E, and T_N climbed slowly but steadily until about 1150 as T_E fluctuated above and below it. By that time the intermittent exposure of the nest was presumably enough to allow solar radiation to heat the sand deeply. After that time T_N remained about the same or increased slightly until 1730, but T_E usually stayed below T_N and fell far below with each wetting. Absences of adults during the hot early afternoon, however, allowed T_E to reach 40° and thus exceed T_N at several points. In this thermocouple-egg the junction was near the upper surface. I attribute the higher and lower T_E's in relation to T_N's to the fact that the thermocouple junction in the egg was at a higher level than the T_N probe and was more subject to rapid solar heating and rapid cooling by wetting, and that water used to cool the eggs was heated in the process and reached the T_N probe level at a higher temperature than when this water was applied to the eggs. After 1600 all temperatures were still high, but T_A and T_N were below 40°, so T_E could be kept between 37° and 39° by a few brief visits to the nest by adult birds. At 1727, a two-minute incubation by a "dry" parent raised T_E from 36° to 37°, suggesting that nest temperatures were still being monitored. By 1800, T_A had dropped to 33.5° but T_N was still 38°, which undoubtedly helped to maintain T_E at 35°. The eggs were now heated from below rather than from above.

In the experiment of 19 March (fig. 5) the thermocouple junction in the egg was centrally located, and fluctuations in T_E were somewhat less rapid. Nevertheless, 19 March was an extremely hot day with shaded T_A's at surface level reaching 46° and higher in the sun. At times I adopted the EP's strategy and went to the river to soak my clothes on the side exposed to the sun. Like the nest monitored on 20 February, this one was more than halfway through incubation and the parent birds were even more closely attentive, especially during the 1030 to 1600 period. All three recorded temperatures (T_A, T_N, T_E) were about the same (38°) at 1000, but at 1016 the first wetting brought T_E down below T_N. From that time until about 1725, T_E usually remained below T_N, but at several points exposure of the nest resulted in T_E's that equalled T_N's, including one up to 41.9° when the presence of people kept the birds off the nest from 1520 to 1529. After 1558 (the time of the last wetting) there were clouds and intermittent sun, and by 1725 T_A had dropped below T_E although T_N remained above, so that by 1800 T_E was still well above T_A but slightly lower than T_N.

During the entire experiment I kept beside me the egg that had been replaced by the thermocouple-egg, buried in unshaded sand with a thermistor probe at egg level, and wetted at times with water from a canteen. The EP's burying-and-wetting system is clearly superior to mine as I had to bury the egg at progressively deeper levels to 120 mm in order to keep the temperature T_{SE} down to 39°. As early as 1030, the temperature around the egg rose to 41° after a five-minute "inattentive period". This egg, which was the smallest of the three and doubtless the last-laid, was returned to the nest, hatched apparently on schedule 11 days later, and produced a vigorous chick that actively joined its siblings and the attending parents.

The detailed temperature data illustrate several points. T_E may vary considerably during the day, demonstrably from 34.0° to 41.9°, without evident harmful effects. Frequent wetting of the eggs is essential to keep T_E's below lethal levels. Shaded T_A's during the hottest hours are well above T_E's and at levels that would be damaging or lethal, so mere shading of the nest would not be adequate to protect the eggs. Heat is retained by the wet sand at the lower level of the eggs, so that after the period of extreme solar heat passes and T_A's decline, the T_E remains within the normal incubation range with little or no parental attentiveness for some time. This unusual reversed temperature gradient (higher to lower from bottom to top of eggs) is therefore adaptive. Temperatures in unshaded dry sand at buried-egg depth reach levels that would

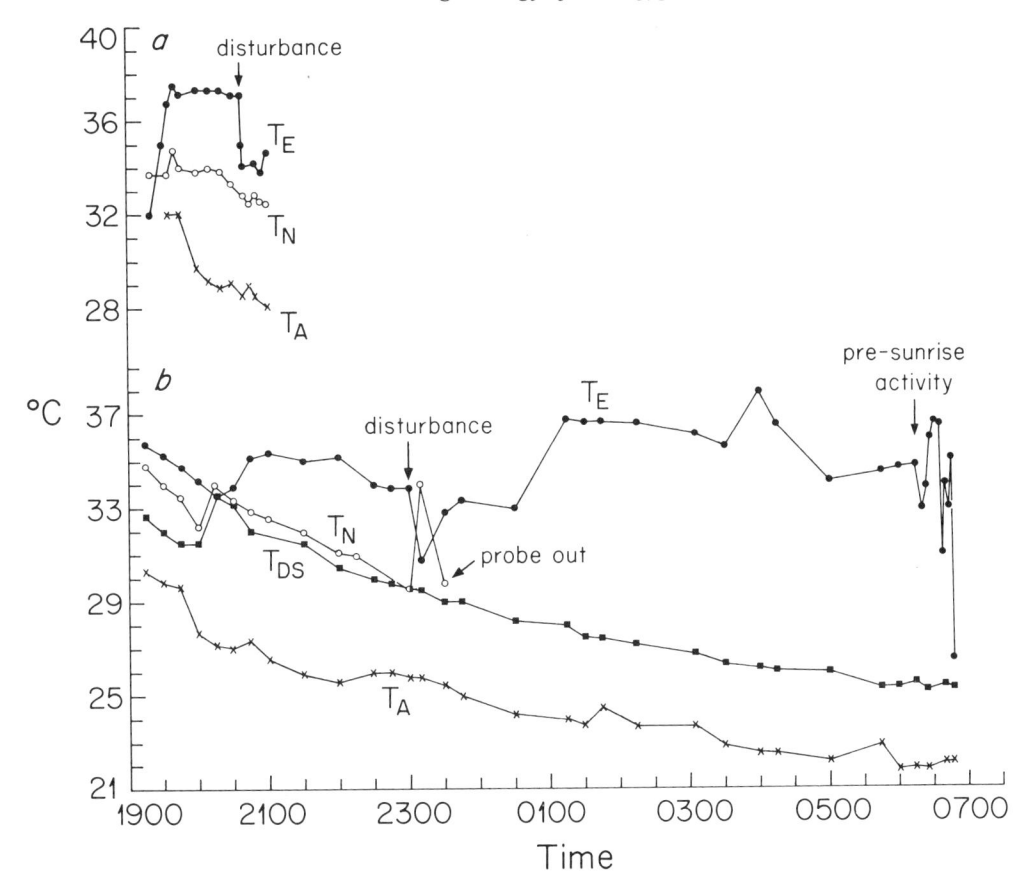

Fig. 6. Ambient, nest, and egg temperatures at night. For definition of symbols see figure 2. Data in part (a) were recorded 1 March 1977; in part (b), 13-14 March 1977. For further details see text.

be lethal for eggs. Therefore the EP could not safely leave its eggs unattended *if unwetted* for more than a few minutes between 1030 and 1600 on any typical day. During these hot hours, the usual temperature relations of incubation are reversed — when the parent attends the nest, the T_E goes down; when the parent leaves the nest, the T_E goes up. In part, then, the eggs of the EP are indeed incubated by solar or environmental heat, but by heat that must be frequently monitored and its effects reduced by continual wetting and covering. During the hottest part of the day it is extremely doubtful that unburied EP eggs, even if wetted by the parents, could maintain temperatures below lethal levels if exposed to full solar radiation for (off) periods as long as those frequently taken by EPs. Water on eggs fully exposed to the sun would quickly evaporate and provide only a brief cooling effect. Only in the early morning and late afternoon is it thermally safe for parent birds to leave the buried eggs unattended for long periods, and this provides them with important free time for foraging and other maintenance activities.

Data from nocturnal monitorings are given in figure 6. On 1 March I went at dusk to the sand-gravel bar on which the nest with the single-egg clutch was located. I added to this nest the thermocouple-egg in which the junction was nearer the egg surface than the center and placed it so that the junction position would be uppermost. A thermistor probe was placed with the tip between the two parallel eggs at about the level (20 mm to 25 mm) of their lower surfaces; the sand at this depth was still slightly damp but it was dry nearer the surface. Recording began at 1920 with T_E and T_A both at 32.0° and below T_N (fig. 6a). It was then too dark to see the nest from a distance, but as T_E rose rapidly it was obvious that a parent bird had returned and was incubating. T_E remained steady between 37.2° and 37.5° from 1930 until 2037. At that point there were loud EP calls at the nest and T_E dropped quickly to around 34° and remained at about that level until the monitoring concluded at 2100. I then went to the nest and found the eggs uncovered for about two-thirds of their depth, much more than was ever the case during the day. The thermocouple-egg had been rotated about 90°, changing the position of the thermocouple junction accordingly. I think that there was either a disturbance or changeover of mates at 2037 that resulted in turning of the thermocouple-egg, or that the egg was turned in the course of foot-excavating by a sitting bird. In any case, the record shows that a bird was on the nest from about 1920 to 2100.

This preliminary experiment was followed by an all-night monitoring of a different nest on 13, 14 March (fig. 6b). This nest had three eggs, the first of which had been laid no later than 2 March (table 1, 4a-c). I replaced the smallest and last-laid egg (4c) with the thermocouple-egg with the junction in the center, and the tip of the probe for recording T_N was placed as before. I buried the removed egg in dry sand at the same depth as the other eggs, and next to it a thermistor probe near its lower surface, about 27 mm down (T_{DS}). Recording began at 1900, which was about the time of sundown. It was too dark to see by the time an EP returned to sit, but the sharp rise in T_E showed that this was between 2000 and 2015. From this point until 2300 T_E remained well above the other temperatures. Just after 2300, some night fishermen with torches came to the island and alarmed the EPs, which called loudly and moved about the nest with some shifting of sand. The T_N probe was evidently pulled to the surface and was close to the bird's incubation patch ($T_N = 34.0°$). Subsequent readings from that probe are omitted in figure 6b. After the fishermen left, an EP resumed incubation as shown by the increase in T_E at 2330. A bird must have been on the nest continuously from then until 0610, when the eastern sky was beginning to lighten and the EPs began calling. Between 0030 and 0130 the thermocouple-egg was apparently more fully uncovered, as T_E rose considerably and remained relatively high. Between 0330 and 0400 the thermocouple-egg must have been maximally in contact with the skin of the incubation patch, as T_E reached 38°. Between 0610 and 0655 there were several change-overs and some alarms caused by kites and people, causing marked fluctuations in T_E and a sharp drop approaching T_{DS} as I terminated the experiment. At this time the nest was dry, the eggs were covered with 2 mm to 3 mm of sand, and the relative position of the thermocouple-egg and the others was unchanged. The thermocouple was still securely cemented into the egg, and all low T_E readings must indicate exposure of the egg to cool air or cool sand. In both nocturnal monitorings of a dry nest with eggs only partly buried, T_E remained consistently above T_N, in contrast to the daytime situation in which fully buried eggs are wetted.

The temperature of the removed egg (table 1, 4c) was presumably the same as T_{DS} (i.e., that of the surrounding sand) after about twelve hours. At 25.3° this was still about 3° above T_A. The egg was then returned to the nest. The other two (4a and 4b) were newly-hatched on the morning of 2 April, but 4c did not hatch and was abandoned by 4 April. This egg may not have been fertile; the contents were addled and lacked indications of blood formation.

The data from this experiment show that the eggs were incubated throughout the night and that they must have been partly uncovered and closely incubated for T_E to reach 38°. Although the temperature (T_{DS}) of buried egg 4c remained consistently about 3° to 4° above T_A, it still declined to less than 30° by 2230 and down to 25.3° by 0650. An egg in advanced stages of development could not survive such prolonged chilling night after night, and it seems certain that EPs must incubate their eggs throughout the night at least during all but the earliest stages. It is possible that fresh eggs (which are much more tolerant of cooling than those at later stages) may not get such continuous nocturnal attendance, but I have no evidence on this point.

In view of the wide range of internal egg temperatures over twenty-four hours, it is difficult to calculate a meaningful mean incubation temperature. The mean of eighty-one T_E's recorded between 1000 and 1800 on 19 March (fig. 5) is 38.67°. Nocturnal T_E's average lower, and I estimate a mean of 36° on undisturbed nights. I propose 37.5° as a reasonable estimate of an overall mean incubation temperature and use this figure in subsequent calculations.

On 2 April, the two newly-hatched chicks from eggs 4a and 4b and the unhatched egg 4c were closely attended by both parents, which regularly wetted them and partly or completely covered them with sand. I placed a bare thermocouple junction in the damp sand of the nest at the level of the underside of the chicks at 1255 and recorded T_N at irregular intervals. Until 1340, T_N varied from 37.5° to 40.0°, with intermittent brooding and wetting. From 1345 to 1525 it varied only from 34.7° to 37.6° as a result of more frequent wettings by each of the parents. At 1525 a parent sat and excavated with its feet, which dislodged the thermocouple. These recordings show that wetting of chicks by the parents is effective in keeping the sand within the range of normal body temperatures. The early post-hatching hours present a critical risk of overheating, and attendance by both parents is probably essential. Later in the day, the chicks may go to the river themselves for drinking and bathing.

PHYSIOLOGY OF INCUBATION

Introductory Review

Commencing especially with the work of Drent (1970) there has been a revival of interest in the physiology of incubation in wild birds. Most notably Rahn and his associates (Rahn and Ar, 1974; Ar et al., 1974; Rahn et al., 1975, 1976, 1977) have studied intensively the influence of temperature, humidity, and shell structure on the changes in egg weight that take place during incubation. The following summary of the work of these authors is brief and therefore inadequate; the references listed above provide full and detailed accounts. (In strictly physical terminology, it is egg mass that changes, and differences in weight are a measure of any change in mass. As practically all of the published studies on changes in egg mass are couched in terms of egg weight, I continue this usage for comparative purposes.)

The egg is heaviest at the time of laying and it loses weight at a fairly constant rate until the shell is fractured by the first pip, after which weight loss increases markedly. The loss in weight is due to the loss of water vapor from the egg contents through microscopic pores in the shell. The porosity characteristics of the shell are presumably genetically determined and species specific but are subject to some intraspecific variation because of the nature of the shell-forming process. The volume of water lost is replaced by the accumulation of air in the air cell at the large end of the egg, providing a means for the near-term chick to initiate pulmonary respiration inside the egg prior to hatching. The amount of water lost (= weight lost) per unit time depends on the porosity of the shell and the differences in water vapor pressure (ΔP_{H_2O}) between the egg contents and the outside medium. The greater this difference, the greater the rate of water loss will be. P_{H_2O} varies with temperature and degree of saturation, so the temperature inside the egg and that surrounding it will influence water loss. As the egg contents are largely fluid, any mixture of gases inside the shell will be saturated (100 percent relative humidity, R.H.) whereas the surrounding medium usually is not. Maximum water loss for a particular egg at a given temperature is achieved if the P_{H_2O} of the surrounding air is zero, as in a desiccator. P_{H_2O}'s at saturation for different temperatures may be obtained from tables of standard physical measurements, so the P_{H_2O} inside the egg can be determined by measuring its internal temperature. The unit of pressure used is the torr, which equals 1/760 of standard atmospheric pressure or 1 mm Hg. (or 133 Pascal in Standard International units).

The water vapor conductance of the shell (G_{H_2O}) is defined as the amount of water lost per day (24 hrs.) per torr. Conductance depends on the porosity of the shell and may differ between species. It can be empirically determined under conditions in which daily (24 hr.) water loss ($\dot{M}_{H_2O}$) and ΔP_{H_2O} can be accurately measured. This can be done by placing the egg in a desiccator in which $P_{H_2O} = 0$, keeping it at a constant temperature, and measuring weight loss each day. The P_{H_2O} inside the egg at that temperature is equal to the ΔP_{H_2O} as the P_{H_2O} outside the egg is zero. Thus,

$$G_{H_2O} = \frac{\dot{M}_{H_2O}}{\Delta P_{H_2O}}$$

Where

G_{H_2O} = water vapor conductance (mg·day^{-1}·torr^{-1})

$\dot{M}_{H_2O}$ = the rate of weight loss (mg·day^{-1})

ΔP_{H_2O} = water vapor pressure difference across the shell (torr)

If G_{H_2O} is known, then one may measure $\dot{M}_{H_2O}$ of eggs in a nest and obtain an estimate of ΔP_{H_2O} (= $\dot{M}_{H_2O}/G_{H_2O}$). If the temperature inside the egg (incubation temperature) and hence its P_{H_2O} is known, then the P_{H_2O} of the nest immediately surrounding the egg can be calculated.

Another method of determination of nest P_{H_2O} involves blowing an egg, filling it with a desiccant such as silica gel, and resealing it (Rahn et al., 1977). The P_{H_2O} inside the egg shell is now zero, and the "silica gel egg" will gain weight when exposed to a medium at higher P_{H_2O}. If such a prepared egg is put in a nest, $\dot{M}_{H_2O}$ now equals weight gained per day = $G_{H_2O} \cdot \Delta P_{H_2O}$. The G_{H_2O} is empirically determined, and ΔP_{H_2O} now equals P_{H_2O} immediately surrounding the prepared egg as P_{H_2O} inside this egg is zero.

Rahn et al. (1974, 1976) have emphasized the importance of the microclimate (temperature and humidity) surrounding the egg in the nest as the gradient between the interior of the egg and its surrounding medium influences water loss. Rahn and Ar (1974) stated, "In desert nesters, one might expect a rather large water vapor gradient; in hole nesters, a relatively small gradient; and among the mound builders [Megapodidae], which cover their eggs with decaying material, no gradient at all and therefore no water loss." Rahn et al. (1977) also emphasized the necessity for the loss of an appropriate fraction of water during incubation.

> The prescribed amount that must be lost during the incubation period can only be achieved if the nest humidity is accurately controlled since the egg temperature is constant as well as the eggshell conductance of water vapor. The precise behavior pattern of the incubating parent which somehow must control the ventilation [of the eggs] in relation to the ambient vapor pressure still needs to be described....

The investigations of Drent and of Rahn, Ar, and their co-workers on the relationship between egg mass, incubation period, water loss, and eggshell conductance prompted me to obtain relevant measurements on the eggs of the EP to ascertain whether or to what extent its egg-burying and egg-wetting habits might introduce variations from the figures predicted by the equations of these authors. Their equations are extremely useful to the field investigator, because deviations from expected values call for a search for adaptive modifications that may be critical for reproductive success under unusual or difficult circumstances.

The data required to test the predictions include duration of the incubation period, incubation temperature, initial (fresh) egg weight, weight loss of eggs in the nest under natural conditions, and weight change of eggs under controlled experimental conditions.

The incubation period and incubation temperatures are discussed on pp. 33-35, 42-51. Initial egg weight can be directly measured only if eggs are discovered on the day of laying, which is particularly difficult in the case of the EP. I found and weighed only four eggs—two in each of two nests—on the day of laying. For eight other eggs that eventually hatched, I determined $\dot{M}_{H_2O}$ in the nest and extrapolated back to the initial weight. To do this, I calculated the probable date of laying from the day of hatching and then the number of days from the calculated date of laying to that of the first weighing. I took the mean daily weight loss from the first to the second weighing, multiplied this by the number of days from laying to first weighing, and added this product to the first weight.

Four other eggs were collected for measurement of weight loss in a desiccator in which the loss was, of course, much higher than in the nest. For these eggs, I could only estimate the date of laying on the basis of field observations at the nest sites before collecting. I found that mean daily weight loss of eggs in nests was 53 percent of mean daily weight loss of eggs in the desiccator, so I multiplied 0.53 times the mean daily weight loss of each of the eggs in the desiccator and multiplied this figure times the estimated number of days post-laying at the time of first weighing. This product was added to that first weight to give an extrapolated initial weight.

Initial egg mass (weight) may also be estimated by the equation

$$W = K_w \cdot L \cdot B^2$$

(Hoyt, 1979)

where

    W = initial weight

    K_W = a constant

    L = egg length

    B = egg breadth at greatest diameter

A mean K_W can be calculated from the data from the four eggs in which W was measured on the day of laying: $K_W = (W/L \cdot B^2) = 0.000547$. The use of this equation yielded estimates of W that were consistently slightly higher than those calculated by my extrapolation method, but the mean weights given by the two methods are not significantly different statistically. Tables 1 and 3 include all of the data discussed above; my preference is to use the extrapolated figures as estimates of initial egg weight. Although individual weights are given to the nearest mg, the mean weight for the EP egg may reasonably be rounded off to 9.5 g.

Koenig (1926) recorded measurements and weights of twenty-six EP eggs collected in Egypt in 1899. The length and breadth dimensions are very similar to those of my eggs, but the weights are generally less (7.0 - 9.3; x̄ = 8.46). Koenig described almost all of his sets of eggs as "fresh," but some of the eggs may have been older than he believed, or possibly his weighing instrument was inaccurate. For example, Koenig (p. 149) recorded an egg that measured 3.1 cm x 2.3 cm and weighed 7.5 g. My egg number 5a in table 1 measured only 2.96 cm x 2.30 cm but weighed 8.51 g on the day of laying. At its measured rate of in-nest weight loss of 0.033 g · day^{-1}, 30 days would be required for a total weight loss of 1 g, down to 7.5 g. I suspect that Koenig's scale was weighing consistently too low.

Adult Body Weight, Egg Weight, and Incubation Period

J. S. Ash has provided me with body weights of EPs captured in mist nets at Gambela. The figures are as follows:

10 ad., 4-14 Dec. 1972, 9-13 Dec. 1973:	73.4-90.5; x̄ = 82.0
6 ad., 19-24 April 1975:	75.2-78.9; x̄ = 76.0
2 ad., 7 first year birds, 13-24 May 1974:	80.5-92.1; x̄ = 86.5

Assuming that food availability was essentially the same in the different years, the data suggest that: (1) the rigors of reproductive activity bring adult body weight to a low point in the latter part of April, when most nesting is over); (2) energy expenditure is much less following nesting, allowing a build-up of body weight in both adults and young, perhaps in preparation for migration or post-breeding dispersal; (3) as the start of the breeding season (January) approaches, mean body weight is lower but still well above the immediate post-nesting weight. I propose 78 g as a reasonable estimate of mean adult body weight at the time that eggs are being produced.

In the EP, the weight of the egg (W) in relation to adult body weight (B) is unusually low in comparison to that of most other charadriiform birds. Using data from a variety of charadriiform species, Rahn et al. (1975) derived the equation $W = 0.61 \cdot B^{0.73}$. This predicts an egg weight for a 78 g EP of 14.67 g instead of the actual 9.5 g. Closer comparison may be made with the true plovers, some of which have values of either W or B similar to those of the EP, using the analyses of Graul (1973) and Jehl (1975) based on twenty species. Jehl's equation for the egg weight-adult body weight relationship in this group is W = 2.93 + 0.14B, which predicts 13.85 g as the egg weight of the EP—close to the figure obtained from the equation of Rahn et al.

Graul (1973) calculated relative egg production (clutch size x W/B) for the twenty plover species; the mean is 0.61. For the EP, using 2.5 as clutch size, the figure is 0.30. In four *Charadrius* species, W is close to that of the EP and in two species B is close; data for these are as follows:

Species	W	B	W/B	Clutch size	Relative egg production
C. hiaticula	11.5	60	0.192	4	0.77
C. semipalmatus	9.6	45	0.213	4	0.85
C. melodus	9.4	52.7	0.178	4	0.71
C. alexandrinus	8.9	43.0	0.206	3	0.62
$\bar{x}$	9.85	50.2	0.197	3.75	0.74
C. leschenaultii	15.6	74.1	0.210	3	0.63
C. modestus	22.0	79.7	0.276	2	0.55
$\bar{x}$	18.8	76.9	0.243	2.5	0.59
Pluvianus aegyptius	9.5	78.0	0.122	2.5	0.30

Compared with these species, the EP has a relatively small egg and apparently puts only one-half as much of its resources into egg production as do plovers of similar body weight.

Within the subfamily Cursoriinae, egg weights of five African species were listed by Schonwetter (1960). J. S. Ash has recorded body weights of mist-netted birds in Ethiopia of three of these, and specimens from Africa of all five species in the Los Angeles County Museum of Natural History include body weight data. The figures are as follows:

Species	W	n(B)	B	W/B	Clutch size	Relative egg production
Cursorius cursor	13.9	10	82	0.170	2	0.34
C. temminckii	8.0	7	62	0.130	2	0.26
Rhinoptilus africanus	9.0	8	69	0.130	1	0.13
R. cinctus	12.1	14	113	0.107	2	0.21
R. chalcopterus	14.0	3	134	0.105	2	0.21

The W/B figures of the latter four species are close to or smaller than that of the EP, showing that relatively small eggs are characteristic of most African coursers, but the EP's incubation period of 30 days is longer than that recorded for any courser regardless of egg weight. The plovers with egg weights close to those of the EP have incubation periods of about 24 days.

Rahn and Ar (1974) plotted incubation period (I) against egg weight for a large, varied sample and derived the equation $I = 12.03 \cdot W^{0.217}$. For the EP's 9.5 g egg this predicts that $I = 19.6$ days. The actual figure of 30 days for an egg of this weight falls outside the 95 percent confidence limits of their equation. Clearly, the EP's incubation period is unusually long and is probably the longest recorded for any egg of this size except among the Storm Petrels (Hydrobatidae: Procellariiformes; Lack, 1967, 1968).

Egg Weight Loss, Conductance, and Water Vapor Pressure in the Nest

To measure daily weight loss under controlled conditions, I made desiccators using half-gallon metal paint cans with airtight lids. I covered the bottom of the can to a depth of several cm with silica gel containing a blue indicator substance that turns colorless as the material becomes hydrated. A few cm above the silica gel I placed a platform of coarse wire mesh on which the egg could be placed without coming in direct contact with the desiccant. The desiccators were tested with a dial-type hygrometer placed inside, and the R.H. read zero. Unfortunately, there was no place available to me in Gambela where temperature could be maintained constant, but inside a well-shaded house the temperature remained at about 26° for about eleven hours during the night, rose to about 30° within two hours after sunrise and, depending on daily conditions, stayed around 30° to 31° (sometimes up to 32°) for about nine hours, and took two hours to decline to 26°. No precise calculation of mean temperature was possible, but I consider 29° a reasonable estimate. The P_{H_2O} inside an egg at this temperature would be about 30 torr. I measured daily weight loss in three eggs under these conditions. Later I was able to put the desiccators in a nonfunctioning refrigerator, and the daily temperature cycle inside this cabinet varied between 28° and 32°. Three different eggs were monitored under these conditions. At an estimated mean temperature of 30°, egg P_{H_2O} would be about 32 torr. Eggs were weighed on a Torsion Balance model DWM2 that could be read to the centigram and estimated to the nearest milligram. Before each weighing, both in the field and indoors, the balance was checked and calibrated with a set of standard precision balance weights.

The results of measurements of the six eggs (from four different nests) are given in table 1. After calculating G_{H_2O} for each egg, I used these figures to calculate for the three eggs at 30 torr what the $\dot{M}_{H_2O}$ would have been at 32 torr. I then used these adjusted figures to calculate a mean $\dot{M}_{H_2O}$ of 0.066 g for all six eggs at 32 torr. $\dot{M}_{H_2O}$ varied slightly in accordance with initial egg weight under identical conditions of temperature and pressure, that is, absolute weight loss per day was generally greater in larger than in smaller eggs. In all six eggs, $\dot{M}_{H_2O}$/initial weight is so close to 0.0072 g that this figure may be assumed to be a constant, which would mean that under these controlled conditions each egg lost an identical average fraction of its initial weight. This in turn suggests that the porosity characteristics of the eggshell of this species are sufficiently uniform that, under ideally constant conditions including identical incubation periods, EP eggs of any size within normal limits would lose exactly the same fraction of their initial weight by the time that hatching was initiated.

G_{H_2O} in these six eggs varied from 1.85 to 2.20, with a mean of 2.08 and a standard deviation of ±0.17. For convenience, the figure may be rounded off to 2.10 mg·day⁻¹· torr⁻¹. G_{H_2O} is thus only relatively constant within a species, and in the case of the EP the variation is attributable to variation in initial egg weight. Ar et al. (1974:54), in their table of G_{H_2O} values, recorded some large standard deviations indicative of considerable intraspecific variation but did not discuss the possible reasons for this.

Ar et al. (1974) used data from twenty-nine species to derive the equation $G_{H_2O} = 0.432 \cdot W^{0.78}$. For the 9.5 g EP egg, G_{H_2O} is predicted as 2.5. The actual figure of about 2.1 is not far below this and not significantly different as it falls well within the 95 percent confidence limits for the equation.

Rahn and Ar (1974) also proposed that the incubation period (I) = $5.2(W/G_{H_2O})$ which indicates that, for a given egg weight, I is inversely proportional to G_{H_2O}, that is, if eggs of two different species have the same weight but one has a much longer incubation period, the egg of that species is expected to have a lower value of G. The equation successfully predicts the different incubation periods of a number of species with similar egg weights. Later studies on twenty-six species of charadriiforms show that a figure of 5.38 instead of 5.2 is more accurate for birds of that order and this yields an equation $G_{H_2O} = 5.38(W/I)$ (Rahn, pers. comm.). Using the actual EP figures for W and I, the equation predicts $G_{H_2O} = 5.38(9.5/30) = 1.70$ which is significantly lower (2 x S.D.) than the mean G_{H_2O} of the EP. The conductance of the eggshell of the EP is therefore about the same as predicted from egg weight alone and significantly higher than that predicted on the basis of weight and incubation period.

As the eggs of the EP in the nest are subjected to conditions ranging from hot and dry to soaking wet, it is obvious that the P_{H_2O} immediately surrounding the eggs is highly variable, in contrast to the controlled experimental conditions described above. To determine weight loss under natural conditions, I measured $\dot{M}_{H_2O}$ in a total of eleven eggs in five different nests (table 1). As expected, $\dot{M}_{H_2O}$ is variable but is also notably low ($\bar{x} = 0.035$ g·day⁻¹).

Using data from forty-six species, Drent (1970) found that the relationship between $\dot{M}_{H_2O}$ during natural incubation and initial egg weight could be expressed as $\dot{M}_{H_2O} = 0.015 \cdot W^{0.74}$. For a 9.5 g EP egg this equation predicts a figure of 0.08 g, or about 2.3 times the observed value. Rahn and Ar (1974) pointed out that FW = $\dot{M}_{H_2O} \cdot I$, where F = the fraction of initial egg weight lost during the course of incubation, and predicted an average value of F of 0.18. If the predicted value of $\dot{M}_{H_2O}$ of 0.08 is used in this equation with W = 9.5 g and I = 30 days, F = > 0.25, or a loss of more than 25 percent of the initial egg weight. It is doubtful that an egg could survive this high degree of water loss, and the EP's 30 day incubation period probably would not be possible without a reduced $\dot{M}_{H_2O}$. Even if F = the average figure of 0.18 and I = 30 days the predicted $\dot{M}_{H_2O}$ would be 0.057 g, which is above the highest figure (0.056 g) actually recorded in a nest and far above the mean. In eight eggs for which I recorded $\dot{M}_{H_2O}$ in the nest and which subsequently hatched, the calculated value for F varied from 0.094 to 0.158 with a mean of 0.114. This is an unusually low figure, and some of the individual F values are among the lowest recorded for any species. Actually, F is something of an abstraction as the equation FW = $\dot{M}_{H_2O} \cdot I$ is valid only as long as $\dot{M}_{H_2O}$ remains relatively constant. Obviously $\dot{M}_{H_2O}$ rises sharply with the first pip, which may occur one or two days before the full hatching in the EP and even longer before in some other species. F will thus be an underestimation of actual water lost prior to hatching but is useful for comparative purposes.

The fact that the G_{H_2O} of the EP egg is not relatively low (and may even be relatively high) indicates that the low $\dot{M}_{H_2O}$ in natural incubation is not attributable to reduced porosity of the shell. This low $\dot{M}_{H_2O}$ must therefore be caused by a low ΔP_{H_2O} between egg and nest. The P_{H_2O} of the EP egg at the mean incubation temperature of 37.5° is about 48 torr, and a low ΔP_{H_2O} therefore means that P_{H_2O} in the nest must approach that relatively high figure. As the EP soaks its eggs for many hours of the day, ΔP_{H_2O} must be close to zero at such times, with little or no water vapor being lost from the egg. At other times, even a covering of relatively dry sand might provide some resistance to diffusion of water vapor through the shell.

To obtain measurements on these points, I blew the contents of one of the eggs (table 1, 6b) used in the desiccator experiments, following standard oölogical methods. I then filled this egg with finely divided silica gel and sealed the opening with quick-drying cement. The egg was calibrated by weighing it before and one or more days after keeping it in a saturated environment. I placed the egg on a wire mesh platform over several cm of water in the bottom of a jar which was then tightly closed and placed in the same cabinet described previously in which mean temperature was about 30°. This exposed the egg to a relative humidity of 100 percent. The method was similar to that of Rahn et al. (1977), except that it was not practical to open the egg and replace the silica gel for repeated calibrations. The prepared egg was placed in a desiccator until it reached a relatively constant low weight and was then placed in an EP nest as soon as possible after the last weighing. It was carried to the nest in a plastic bag containing a packet of silica gel so that weight gain in transit, if any, would be extremely low. The EPs tested gave no indication of treating this experimental egg any differently from their own. (Data from a second silica-gel egg had to be discarded as the egg cracked at some unknown time.)

The weight gains of the intact silica-gel egg when placed in two different nests and when placed in the hydrator jar are given in table 3. In an egg this small, internal P_{H_2O} builds up sufficiently during hydration so that water vapor influx is progressively reduced (Rahn et al., 1977), and the figures for first-day weight gains when initial egg weight is lowest are the most reliable. The figure of 0.068 g in the hydrator on 18 to 19 March is very close to the adjusted mean twenty-four hour weight loss of 0.069 g for the same egg in the desiccator at the same mean temperature and thus at about the same ΔP_{H_2O}. Using the figure of 0.068 g, the G_{H_2O} of the egg equals 2.12. The G_{H_2O} of this same egg calculated when unblown was 2.17. The closeness of these weight change and conductance values indicates that the porosity characteristics of the shell were not importantly changed by the preparation process. I have used 2.15 as the mean G_{H_2O} for calculations involving this egg.

In the first nest tested, I was able to weigh the egg after a span of sixteen hours from 1800 to 1000, during which it was almost certainly not wetted; then after seven hours during most of which time the nest presumably was actively wetted; then after about twenty-four hours during which time the nest presumably was actively wetted for about six hours and not wetted for about eighteen hours. Later, I recorded weight gain after nine hours, during most of which time the egg presumably was actively wetted, and fifteen hours during which it was not. I did not continuously monitor activities at these nests while the silica-gel egg was in place, but presume that the wetting schedule followed the typical daily pattern. If weight gain per hour is calculated, the figures for the two actively wetted periods are very close; those for the "dry" periods

TABLE 3
Silica Gel Egg Data

Date	Time	Wt(g)	±Wt(g)	No. Hrs In Nest	$\bar{x} \pm Wt \cdot hr^{-1}$(mg)	Condition of Nest
9 March	1800	8.095	—	—	—	unwetted
10 March	1000	8.105	0.010	16	0.6	unwetted
10 March	1715	8.129	0.024	7.25	3.4	wetted for most of time
11 March	1800	8.196	0.067	24.75	2.7	presumably wetted for 6 hrs, then not for 18
17 March	0900	8.162	—	—	—	nest initially dry
17 March	1800	8.194	0.032	9	3.5	slightly damp, actively wetted earlier
18 March	0900	8.224	0.030	15	2.0	unwetted
18 March	1745	8.212	-0.012	8.75	-1.3	abandoned, dry, exposed to sun; egg then placed in hydrator (see 19-20 March)
2 April	1700	8.400	—	—	—	nest slightly damp
3 April	1530	8.448	0.048	22.5	2.1	slightly damp; presumably wetted earlier

In Hydrator

						$\bar{x}T_A$,°C	$\bar{x}P_{H_2O}$, torr
19 March	1830	8.280	0.068	24.75	2.7	30	32
20 March	1730	8.330	0.050	23	2.2	30	32

are not as close but average 0.0013 g·hr^{-1} (table 3). Multiplying this figure by twenty-four hours, the daily weight gain in an unwetted nest would be 0.0312 g = $\dot{M}_{H_2O}$. As G_{H_2O} of this egg = about 2.15, the ΔP_{H_2O} = (31.2 mg/2.15) = 14.5 torr = P_{H_2O} of the dry nest. If a natural egg at 37.5°C and a P_{H_2O} of 48 torr were present in such a nest, the ΔP_{H_2O} would equal 33.5. Substituting this figure in the equation $\dot{M}_{H_2O}$ = G_{H_2O} (2.15) · ΔP_{H_2O} (33.5), $\dot{M}_{H_2O}$ = 0.072 g. This is within the limits of the range of daily variation of empirically determined twenty-four hour water loss of this and other natural eggs in the desiccator at a mean ΔP_{H_2O} of 32 instead of 33.5 torr. If 32 is substituted for 33.5, $\dot{M}_{H_2O}$ = 68.8 mg, which is quite close to the mean desiccator $\dot{M}_{H_2O}$ of 66 mg and indicates that the values obtained from the silica-gel egg are consistent with those from natural eggs. The figure of 0.072 g is also not very different from 0.0786 g as predicted by Drent's equation $\dot{M}_{H_2O}$ = 0.015 · $W^{0.74}$ if the estimated initial weight of this egg (9.368 g) is used. If a natural egg of initial weight 9.368 g lost weight at 0.072 g for 30 days, the total weight loss would be 2.160 g, and F = >0.23 or more than 23 percent of the initial egg weight.

A value of F as high as 0.23 has not been recorded for successfully hatching eggs of any charadriiform species in nature. No extensive lists of F values have been published.

but approximate values may be calculated for some of the species listed in Drent's (1970) appendix, which gives daily weight loss and fresh egg weight, and Lack's (1967) Appendix I which gives incubation periods for many of these species. Among species of procellariiform, pelecaniform, and charadriiform birds in which I = 30 days or more, F ranges only from 0.12 to 0.18. (In Drent's list, *Sula sula* is a misprint for *S. bassana*.) In the seven species of terns studied by Rahn et al. (1976), F ranges from 0.12 to 0.16. In view of the available evidence, I doubt that an EP egg in nature could survive a fractional water loss of 0.23, and in the EP population that I studied, the natural value of F was never close to 0.23 because $\dot{M}_{H_2O}$ did not average 0.072 g but only 0.035 g.

The figures for mean hourly weight gain of the silica-gel egg in the nest while wetted are slightly higher than those obtained in the hydrator at saturation. This is probably because the temperature of the wet sand immediately around the eggs averages about 37.5°, and P_{H_2O} of the nest when fully wetted would be 48 torr rather than 32 torr as in the hydrator at 30°.

The total 24.75 hour weight gain of the silica-gel egg in the nest between 10 and 11 March was 0.067 g. Substituting this figure and the G_{H_2O} of this egg in the equation $(\dot{M}_{H_2O}/G_{H_2O}) = \Delta P_{H_2O}$, the latter equals 31.2 torr. As the silica-gel egg is at $P_{H_2O} = 0$, 31.2 torr must equal the mean nest P_{H_2O} over twenty-four hours. If a normal egg were in the nest at 37.5° and P_{H_2O} of 48 torr, ΔP_{H_2O} would be 48-31.2 = 16.8 torr. Using the same equation and substituting mean $\dot{M}_{H_2O}$ and G_{H_2O} figures for normal eggs under natural incubation, the predicted ΔP_{H_2O} of (35 mg/2.1) = 16.6 torr, essentially identical to that calculated from silica-gel egg data. Mean nest P_{H_2O} would be 31.4 torr at this ΔP_{H_2O}, and 31.3 torr is the mean between the two calculations of ΔP_{H_2O}. The mean nest P_{H_2O} for an unwetted nest over a twenty-four hour period calculated from silica-gel egg data would be 14.5 torr (p. 59), and at this nest P_{H_2O} the predicted $\dot{M}_{H_2O}$ for twenty-four hours would be 0.072 g, or 3 mg·hr^{-1}. The empirically determined mean $\dot{M}_{H_2O}$ of eggs in naturally incubated nests with a mean P_{H_2O} of 31.3 torr is 0.035 g, or (35 mg/24) = about 1.4 mg·hr^{-1}. If the nest is kept soaked for about six hours out of twenty-four, as field observations indicate, then nest P_{H_2O} would be 48 torr during that interval and no water vapor would then be lost from the eggs. Thus, the entire $\dot{M}_{H_2O}$ of 35 mg would be lost over eighteen hours rather than twenty-four. At times when the (unwetted) mean nest P_{H_2O} was 14.5 torr the rate of water loss would be 3 mg·hr^{-1}, and the nest P_{H_2O} at other times would vary between 48 and 14.5 torr with a mean of 31.25 (= 31.3) torr and a mean hourly water loss of 1.4 mg. If x = number of hours out of eighteen when water loss·hr^{-1} = 1.4 mg and y = number of hours at 3 mg·hr^{-1}, then 1.4x + 3y = 35 mg. As y = 18 - x, solving the equation gives approximate values of x = 12 hours and y = 6 hours. One may then suggest spans of different mean nest P_{H_2O} as follows:

$$\longleftarrow \underset{6 \text{ hrs}}{\bar{x} = 48 \text{ torr}} \times \underset{12 \text{ hrs}}{\bar{x} = 31.3 \text{ torr}} \times \underset{6 \text{ hrs}}{\bar{x} = 14.5 \text{ torr}} \longrightarrow .$$

The spans would not necessarily be in that continuous sequence and the demarcations would not be sharp, but these figures would give a twenty-four hour mean of 31.3 torr for nest P_{H_2O}. (This is mathematically inevitable since (48 + 14.5) ÷ 2 = 31.3, but P_{H_2O}s of those values for those time spans correspond well with the field measurements and observations, indicating that the use of these mean figures does not conceal large intra-interval fluctuations.) As R.H. at a given temperature = (actual P_{H_2O}/P_{H_2O} at saturation) the mean R.H. in the nest over twenty-four hours would be (31.3/48) = about 65 percent, a high average figure that presumably results from the many hours at an R.H. of 100 percent. It is this high degree of saturation of the sand surrounding the eggs that is responsible for the low $\dot{M}_{H_2O}$ of 0.035 g·day^{-1} in naturally incubated eggs. As an aid to information retrieval, most of the data discussed above are summarized in table 4.

The wetting of the nest and eggs is essential to keep egg temperature below the lethal level, and the data above show that this wetting may also be necessary to prevent excessive water loss over the long incubation period of 30 days. In view of the generally low $\dot{M}_{H_2O}$ and F values in the EP egg, the suggestion of Rahn et al. (1974) that the hatching process may not be initiated until an appropriate fraction of water has been lost should be examined. The data from the monitored nests provide some information for evaluation of this hypothesis. The natural F values, while generally low, show a wide range. Eggs 3a and 3b in a clutch of two had F values of 15.8 percent and 10.0 percent respectively, yet both were pipped on the same day and presumably hatched on the next (but see below). The two most thoroughly monitored eggs, 4a and 4b, had the lowest F values. Presumably, F has lower and upper limits, which may be determined as follows. The lower limit would be the minimal fraction of water that must be lost if the physiological processes of embryonic development are to continue normally, and this would correspond closely to the minimal volume of the air cell that would allow adequate pre-hatching ventilation of the respiratory tract. The upper limit would be the maximum fraction of water that could be lost without pathological effects of dehydration; the resulting more-than-adequate air cell would not necessarily be advantageous but presumably would not have deleterious effects. Thus, the egg could tolerate a range of water loss corresponding to that imposed by the inevitable irregularities associated with incubation in nature.

As an example of the latter, I will cite details in the case of egg number 2, table 1. This single egg was placed in a more gravelly substrate than is usual for the EP. The mean $\dot{M}_{H_2O}$ after an estimated five days post-laying was 27 mg; the mean $\dot{M}_{H_2O}$ nine days later was 47 mg. At the next weighing six days later I detected a small, slight, depressed fracture; none of the shell was missing and the fracture was probably caused by a parent bird shifting the egg in the gravelly nest. The mean $\dot{M}_{H_2O}$ over that six day period was 65 mg. In calculating F as 0.128 as given in table 1, I used the approximate mean $\dot{M}_{H_2O}$ (40 mg) of the first two means on the assumption that 65 mg was abnormally high because of the fracture. If actual weight loss is calculated assuming an $\dot{M}_{H_2O}$ of 65 mg for the eight days between the last weighing and hatching, F would be about 0.158. The newly-hatched chick seemed normal in size and activity, but unfortunately this island was flooded by a rise in the river four days later and the chick disappeared. Eggs 3a and 3b were in a substrate only slightly less gravelly on an adjacent island. It is conceivable that egg 3b, which had an unusually high $\dot{M}_{H_2O}$ and the highest F value, may have experienced some minute shell cracking that was not detectable to the fingertip or the unaided eye.

The long incubation period and its possible determinants and adaptive value will be treated in the Discussion section.

TABLE 4
Summary of Data on Egg Weight Changes and P_{H_2O} of Nest

Natural initial weight (W) of egg later filled with silica gel	9.368 g
Conductance (G_{H_2O}), silica gel egg	2.15 mg · day^{-1} · torr^{-1}
Mean weight gain per hour, silica gel egg, unwetted nest	1.3 mg
Calculated $\dot{M}_{H_2O}$, silica gel egg, unwetted nest: 24 × 1.3	31.2 mg
Silica gel egg ($P_{H_2O} = 0$) in unwetted nest: $\Delta P_{H_2O} = \dfrac{\dot{M}_{H_2O}}{G_{H_2O}} = \dfrac{31.2}{2.15} = P_{H_2O}$ of unwetted nest	14.5 torr
Natural egg P_{H_2O}, incubation temperature 37.5°C	48.0 torr
ΔP_{H_2O}, natural egg in unwetted nest: 48.0 - 14.5	33.5 torr
Predicted $\dot{M}_{H_2O}$, natural egg, unwetted nest: $\dot{M}_{H_2O} = G_{H_2O} \cdot \Delta P_{H_2O} = 2.15 \cdot 33.5$	72.0 mg
Predicted total weight loss, natural egg in hypothetical unwetted nest: I (30 days) · $\dot{M}_{H_2O}$ (72 mg)	2.160 g
Predicted fraction (F) of initial weight (W) lost: $\dfrac{2.160}{9.368}$	0.23
Silica gel egg in naturally wetted nest: 24.75 hour weight gain (approx. $\dot{M}_{H_2O}$)	67.0 mg
$\Delta P_{H_2O} = \dfrac{67}{2.15}$ = mean natural nest P_{H_2O}	31.2 torr
Natural egg in naturally wetted nest: $\Delta P_{H_2O} = \dfrac{35}{2.10} = 16.6$; mean natural nest $P_{H_2O} = 48 - 16.6$	31.4 torr
Mean of both calculations	31.3 torr
Predicted water loss per hour, natural egg, unwetted nest: $\dfrac{72}{24}$	3 mg · hr^{-1}
Measured water loss per hour, natural egg, natural nest: $\dfrac{35}{24}$	1.4 mg · hr^{-1}

SHELL THICKNESS AND WEIGHT

Measurements of shell thickness of ten eggs for which initial weight was either recorded or calculated are given in table 1. These eggshells were brought from Gambela and measured with a micrometer device and a Mettler precision balance at the oölogical study facilities of the Western Foundation of Vertebrate Zoology, Los Angeles, California. The figures for mean thickness and mean initial weight of entire eggs may reasonably be rounded off to 0.20 mm and 9.230 g. Ar et al. (1974) assumed that shell thickness is an index of the length (L) of the pores and calculated the regression L (in μ) = $5.126 \cdot 10^{-3} \cdot W^{0.456}$ based on data from 367 species. Substituting the mean of 9.230 for W in this equation yields a prediction for L of 142μ (= 0.142 mm). The actual mean thickness of 0.20 mm is higher than the predicted L but within the 95 percent confidence limits of the equation.

Although actual mean shell thickness is within the statistically significant limits of prediction on the basis of egg weight, in my sample of ten eggs the thickness of individual eggshells is not strongly correlated with initial egg weight, that is, heavier (larger) eggs may have thinner shells than lighter (smaller) ones and vice versa, even within the same clutch (table 1, 5a, 5b; 7b, 7c). Shell weight is not strongly correlated with initial egg weight either, but shell thickness and shell weight are 100 percent correlated in this sample. Thicker shells are heavier than the next thickest although the latter may be from eggs of greater initial weight and larger external dimensions (table 1, 5a, 5b; 8, 9a). The data thus indicate that in the EP there is considerable individual variation in shell thickness independent of initial egg weight and overall size. This raises the question of whether shell thickness, which presumably determines pore length, affects the water vapor conductance of the shell. In only three of my eggs (table 1, 6b, 7a, 8) do I have measurements both of shell thickness and conductance. It happens that these three eggshells had, in order of increasing thickness, the three highest conductance values. The sample is too small and the differences too slight to be significant, though, and the most that can be said is that these figures give no indication that an increase in shell thickness is necessarily accompanied by a decrease in conductance.

Paganelli, Olszowka, and Ar (1974) related shell weight to initial weight by the equation $W_{shell} = 4.82 \cdot 10^{-2} \cdot W^{1.132}$. Substituting in this equation the mean initial weight (9.282) for the six eggs for which I have shell weights yields a predicted W_{sh} of 0.60 g. The actual mean weight for these six shells is 0.731 g but the figure is within the 95 percent conficence limits of the equation.

Although my sample of egg shells from Gambela is small, the means for shell thickness (0.20 mm), weight (0.731 g), and shell weight relative to initial egg weight (7.85 percent) correspond closely to the figures for these respective categories (0.18 mm; 0.80 g; 7.8 percent) reported by Schönwetter (1960) for *Pluvianus*. There is thus no reason to suppose that the characteristics of the Gambela sample are outside the normal limits of the species as a whole. In summary, the data on eggshell thickness and weight do not provide any evidence of structural modifications at the macroscopic level that might account for the unusually low rate of daily water loss in the EP egg.

Table 5 summarizes all the predictive equations tested, the predicted values, and the empirically determined mean values of characteristics relevant to the physiology of incubation in the EP.

TABLE 5

Summary of Predicted and Actual Mean Values of Characteristics Relevant to the Physiology of Incubation in *Pluvianus aegyptius*

Characteristic	Predictive equation	Predicted value	Actual mean value	Statistically significant difference
Adult body weight (B)	—	—	78 g	—
Initial egg weight (W)	$W = 0.61 \cdot B^{0.73}$	14.7 g	9.5 g	yes
Incubation period (I)	$I = 12.03 \cdot W^{0.217}$	19.6 days	30 days	yes
Daily water loss of egg ($\dot{M}_{H_2O}$)	$\dot{M}_{H_2O} = 0.015 \cdot W^{0.74}$	0.08 g	0.035 g	yes
Fraction (F) of W lost during I	$F = \dfrac{\dot{M}_{H_2O} \cdot I}{W}$	0.23	0.114	yes
Eggshell conductance (G_{H_2O})	$G_{H_2O} = 0.432 \cdot W^{0.78}$	2.5 mg·day^{-1}·torr^{-1}	2.1 mg·day^{-1}·torr^{-1}	no
Eggshell thickness (L)	$L = 5.126 \cdot 10^{-3} \cdot W^{0.456}$	0.142 mm	0.20 mm	no
Eggshell weight (W_{sh})	$W_{sh} = 4.82 \cdot 10^{-2} \cdot W^{1.132}$	0.60 g	0.731 g	no

See table 1 and text for details of measurements and for references.

Chick Weight

Six chicks were weighed on the day of hatching with a Pesola dynamometer, and the weights ranged from 7.0 to 7.5 g (table 1). The mean calculated initial weight of these six eggs was 9.72 g, and the mean chick weight of 7.23 g is 74.4 percent of that figure. I was unable to weigh chicks on successive days after hatching.

Fledging Period

This term is sometimes defined with reference to the acquisition of the first set of contour feathers or to the young bird's first use of them for flight. I use the term here to mean the period between hatching and the young bird's first self-initiated, effective flight. By effective flight I mean one in which the bird launches itself into the air and then effectively prolongs the airborne interval by the active use of its wings. I use self-initiated flight as opposed to one prompted prematurely by a predator or other external disturbance. In nidicolous birds that nest above ground (and especially in cavities) this period can be fairly accurately determined under favorable circumstances, but in nidifugous ground-nesters its determination can be difficult or impossible (Lack, 1968:211). Nevertheless, best approximations of fledging period are worthwhile for comparative purposes.

I did not see any EP juveniles fly by 6 April, the time of my departure. The oldest juveniles that I saw regularly had hatched on 5 or 6 March and I last saw them on 4 April. When alarmed they sometimes raised their wings slightly while running but did not take flight although they seemed about to do so. I believe they would have been able to fly spontaneously within a few more days, and I estimate the fledging period to be not less than 30 days and probably about 35 days.

DISCUSSION

With the foregoing sections as background, I now compare the reproductive biology of the EP with that of other birds to which it is most similar, to seek out the potential adaptive value of the EP's more unusual habits, and to suggest possible evolutionary pathways that led to these.

The burying of eggs by the EP is more highly developed than in any other charadriiform species but does not resemble the monumental mound-building behavior of the Megapodidae. Chick-burying by the EP after the young have left the nest appears to be unique among birds. All of the EP's unusual habits, however, are extensions of behavior patterns found to some extent in various other charadriiforms, particularly other coursers and some true plovers.

Maclean (1974) reviewed the practice of egg-covering in the Charadrii, including original observations and extensive references. In this group, egg-covering has been recorded in four families: Jacanidae, Glareolidae, Charadriidae, and Thinocoridae. Members of the first and last of these cover the eggs with pieces of vegetation used as nest material; only some of the glareolids and charadriids cover the eggs with sand or soil. Glareolids use the bill to toss the sand whereas charadriids use the feet. Among the four *Charadrius* species in which egg-covering is reported, *C. pecuarius* (Hall, 1958, 1959; Conway and Bell, 1968) and *C. marginatus* (Hall, 1960) are the best known. *C. pecuarius* covers the eggs only when departing in alarm; they are uncovered as the bird resumes incubation. Newly-hatched chicks in the nest may also be partly covered along with unhatched eggs. In *C. marginatus* egg-covering is also done only in alarm, is usually less complete than in *C. pecuarius,* and shows more individual variation in the extent of covering and uncovering. Hall (1960) used a mercury-bulb thermometer to record temperatures of shaded air and sand around buried eggs in *C. marginatus,* presumably soon after flushing the incubating bird. He found little difference between the two temperatures and no indication that egg burial played a definite role in thermoregulation. Most of the temperatures recorded were in a range of 15° to 25°C, which indicates that the nest sites were not under heat stress at the times of measurement.

Kemp and Maclean (1973) studied a nest of the Three-banded Courser (*Rhinoptilus cinctus*) in which the eggs were kept almost (but never completely) buried in soil even while being incubated, but they were not equipped to record temperatures in the nest and did not see the circumstances of the initial burial. Archer and Godman (1937) also recorded partial egg-burial in this species.

Cooling of the eggs or chicks by wetting from water-soaked ventral feathers of parent birds has been reported in many charadriiform species, but temperature measurements are rare. Maclean (1975) reviewed charadriiform soaking behavior and found that it has not been recorded in coursers other than the EP, perhaps because the other courser species usually nest in dry areas where surface water is rarely available.

George Kainady and Al-Dabbagh (1976) documented ventral feather-soaking and nest-wetting by *Charadrius alexandrinus* in a hot desert environment in Iraq, and their paper includes numerous soil surface and air temperatures and a single temperature (44°C) taken in a nest "soon after" the parent bird left. They interpreted the frequent soakings primarily as a means of heat loss by the adult birds, but their observations also make clear that the (unburied) eggs and the nest site were wetted. Roberts (1977) briefly reported seeing *C. marginatus* wet its sand-covered eggs with its soaked ventral feathers under "very hot" conditions. Gatter (1971) published excellent photographs showing ventral feather-soaking and wetting of chicks by *Charadrius dubius.* Despite the paucity of published nest temperature measurements, there can be no reasonable doubt that many charadriiform birds that nest in hot situations cool the eggs and sometimes the chicks by wetting them. At the same time, soaking by the adult birds is a way of losing body heat, and wetting the eggs may prevent excessive water loss if nest humidity is otherwise very low. All of these potential advantages are not mutually exclusive but are collectively beneficial, conferring high selective value on the behavior pattern. Except for the sandgrouse and the EP, however, soaking and water transport seem to be carried out on an ad hoc basis depending on local conditions.

The EP is of special interest because its distinctive egg-burying, ventral soaking and nest-wetting, and chick-burying are highly developed, species-specific characteristics involving stereotyped behavior patterns, all of which are evidently essential to reproductive success. To review each of these:

EGG-BURYING

There are no reliable reports of EP nesting in which the full clutch of eggs was not largely or completely buried during the day whenever the parents were absent. During the day the eggs appear to remain buried even when a sitting bird is present and a normal clutch has never been found fully uncovered. Data in previous sections show the importance of egg-burying by the EP for concealment and for thermoregulation. As several species of plovers conceal their eggs by covering with sand but without demonstrable thermal benefits, it seems highly probable that concealment was the original adaptive value of egg-burying by the EP and that thermoregulatory advantages developed as burying became more thorough. The eggs of the EP are cryptically colored, a characteristic presumably retained from open-nesting ancestors.

Soaking and Nest-Wetting

The highly stereotyped soaking behavior commences only with the laying of the first egg. Because both sexes show identical soaking patterns at the start of incubation, the initiation of the behavior is probably not attributable to gonadal hormone changes as these would not be expected at that time in the male. Although soaking and nest-wetting appear to be programmed activities, they may be suspended in the absence of heat stress. This indicates that the behavior requires both endogenous and exogenous stimuli for expression. EPs do not soak themselves except before going to the nest and eggs, indicating that soaking and nest-wetting are coupled and that soaking is not merely a comfort activity that coincidentally aids in nest temperature regulation. There is evidence that the birds monitor nest temperature, and nest-wetting during the hot hours takes on the appearance of a compulsion. Even with people or potential predators close by the nest, the parent birds will soak and return to it although showing extreme nervousness. Going to the nest under such circumstances is risky as it reveals the hidden location, but opposed to this risk is the certainty that the eggs will be destroyed by overheating if not wetted. Selection would therefore favor a strong drive to wet the eggs under hot conditions, despite clear and present dangers.

Chick-Burying

This behavior is presumably derived from egg-burying, but its prolongation until the chicks are at least three weeks of age is remarkable. As incubation must begin with the laying of the first egg, hatching is not entirely synchronous and the parents must continue to care for unhatched eggs in the usual manner even after the first chick is present. The newly-hatched chick is inevitably covered over along with the remaining egg(s) while it stays in the nest (as sometimes happens in *Charadrius pecuarius*). In the EP neither eggs nor chicks are deeply covered, and a quiet chick can doubtless obtain adequate oxygen under loose sand for many minutes. If it begins to suffer anoxia, it can easily raise its head or entire body above the sand. From burying newly-hatched chicks along with eggs in the nest, it is not a great step to continuation of chick-burying when danger threatens even after they have left the nest. As young birds do not fly until at least four weeks of age and thus may be confined to a small sandbar for that time, it is probably advantageous to retain the chick-covering behavior pattern as long as possible. Wetting of buried chicks outside the nest is doubtless an extension of the egg-wetting pattern, and it is done in the same manner with the soaked ventral feathers. I have previously (p. 41) discussed Butler's (1931) account of chick-wetting by regurgitation and why I believe it to be a misinterpretation.

More remarkable, perhaps, than the burying activity of the adults is the continuing tolerance of the chicks to complete and repeated burials and their inertness while being dug out and exposed. The chicks are cryptically colored when their white wings are folded and the head retracted so that the black and white nape pattern is concealed. This is the posture assumed when crouching in a depression in the sand, and remaining immobile in such a position as danger approaches is characteristic of virtually all species of cryptically patterned young birds. In the EP, the adult further conceals its offspring with a covering of sand; the young bird not only remains immobile if touched but also if excavated out of the sand, picked up, and handled. This seems to represent the ultimate degree to which crypsis may be used as a defensive strategy for young birds. The uncovered chick is inconspicuous, a partly-covered chick is even less conspicuous, and a fully-covered chick is invisible. The price of such invisibility is that escape by sudden movement is impossible. Hence, there is a high selective premium on maintaining immobility even while being excavated. A chick that struggled as a predator probed to find it would have little chance of escape, whereas the predator might abandon its efforts if it missed the exact location of the chick or encountered only an inert object under the sand. In the last extremity after being dug out, the startling effect of quick, strong movement by a previously immobile young bird would probably offer the best possibility for escape. This strategy worked well against me while I photographed my stepwise excavation of a buried juvenile and assumed for too long that it would not suddenly leap up and run away.

Adult Plumage Pattern

The concealment of the eggs and cryptic patterning of the chicks contrasts strikingly with the extreme conspicuousness of the adult birds from every angle of view. I found this to be the case whether I looked directly down on an adult EP from a high river bank, or watched one from ground level, or observed one from anywhere in between. I expected that the bold patterning of the EP would serve to disrupt its outlines against the background of its nesting or foraging sites, as in some other coursers and many of the ringed plovers, but this was not so. There was no situation in which I found the EP's pattern to be concealing, and a stationary EP is seldom more conspicuous than when sitting on a nest in the open on a wide expanse of sand. Maximum conspicuousness is reached during flight or during threat displays, when the flashing black and white pattern of the wings and tail is exposed. Presumably there are advantages to such conspicuousness that outweigh those that might be provided by concealing coloration.

The most obvious advantage to any conspicuous patterning is its use as a social signal, especially to conspecific individuals. In many species it facilitates rapid species recognition and location of other individuals, especially potential mates, and striking patterns are often used in courtship or aggressive display as in territorial defense. I doubt that there has been strong selection pressure for conspicuousness in the EP in association with any of these activities except aggressive display. Recognition and location of conspecific individuals probably would not pose serious problems for the EP even if it were highly cryptic. Its populations are distributed extensively and exclusively along rivers and are thus readily encountered, and none of its close relatives occurs in this habitat. Its vocalizations are also loud and distinctive. The sexes are indistinguishable in plumage and courtship displays seem to be virtually minimal. On the other hand, threat displays are visually striking and territorial defense is vigorous and uses such displays prominently. Greater conspicuousness probably enhances the chance of acquiring and maintaining a breeding territory and thus has been favored by selection.

The drawback of conspicuousness in both sexes is that adults may attract the attention of predators to themselves and to their nest. Some conspicuous birds nest only in predator-free locations. Other conspicuous species are usually found in habitats where they can quickly take cover, or are large and strong enough to discourage attacks, or associate in large groups that can repel predators, or if relatively small and solitary are extremely aggressive. The EP clearly falls in the last category.

Both sexes of the EP strongly defend their breeding territory, not only against conspecifics but against all potential predators and competitors, and they do this continuously for at least three months. The most probable benefit of this great expenditure of energy would be to discourage predators and, by expelling competitors, to assure an adequate food supply for the offspring, which may be confined to the nesting island for at least four weeks after hatching. My observations have persuaded me that successful territorial defense requires participation of both sexes, and that the effectiveness of defense is greatly enhanced by the birds' conspicuous and distinctive coloration. A threat display or the flash of black and white wings at the start of a flight often seems enough to rout an intruder. Sometimes one EP holds a predator's attention in front by threat displays while the mate flies up and strikes the predator from behind (pl. 4). It is possible that the conspicuous presence of an EP on its territory may discourage intrusions by smaller birds that are sure to be driven off.

Whether or not conspicuousness provides such benefits, the cost is increased risk of revealing the location of the nest. This risk is minimized by the highly developed nest-covering behavior. Despite its general aggressiveness, the EP's strategy is usually not to stand fast and defend the nest itself but to cover it quickly, move away, and then distract the predator by making false nest scrapes, or giving threat displays, or by attacking it—in short, to be conspicuous away from the nest. My hypothesis is that the benefits of conspicuousness as outlined above must be greater than the cost. I can think of no other reasons why a relatively small, nondimorphic, vulnerable bird that nests solitarily on highly exposed sites should not only lack cryptic patterning but should be positively striking in appearance.

Incubation Period and Fledging Period

Related to the costs of conspicuousness at the nest is the matter of the unusually long, 30 day incubation period. Considering the risks to a nest in the open such as that of the EP, one would expect this species to have the shortest possible incubation period compatible with the production of precocial young, yet this seems not to be the case. For example, some medium-small plovers and the quail *Coturnix coturnix* have eggs of about the same size as the EP and hatch equally precocial chicks with about one to two weeks less incubation time, respectively. Adequate discussion of this point requires a review of the data on incubation and fledging periods.

The factors that determine incubation period are not fully known, but the avian embryonic system obviously requires a minimum time for development within the egg from the zygote to a stage of readiness to hatch. This minimum period is presumably fixed by genetically determined rates of physiological processes as well as by the amount of nutrients and other essential materials available to the embryo within the shell, which may in turn reflect the physiological resources of the female parent at the time of laying. The minimum degree of development needed for hatching and subsequent survival must include the ability to pierce the shell membrane into the air cell and ventilate the complex respiratory system prior to breaking through the shell and emerging from it. Except for rare and possibly equivocal cases, no bird species is known to be able to achieve the necessary minimum degree of development in less than about 11 days (Nice, 1954a, 1954b; Skutch, 1976). The scarcity of authentic instances of 10 day incubation periods emphasizes the generality of the 11 day lower limit. This lower limit is attained only in altricial birds; precocial species, no matter how small, have longer incubation periods and the shortest known is that of *Turnix,* which (in captivity, at least) may be only 12 days (Hoesch, 1960; Flieg, 1973).

The fledging period (p. 65) is usually less well-demarcated than the incubation period but is significant because for most species attainment of the ability to fly effectively is the most important single event after hatching in terms of future survival. The time required for fledging also has a lower limit, represented by the time needed to develop adequate feathering and the neuromuscular coordination and power necessary for effective flight. Heinroth (1922), and later Lack (1948), noted a general correlation between incubation and fledging periods. The compilations provided by Lack (1948, 1967, 1968), Kendeigh (1952), and Skutch (1976) are convenient sources of information on these periods. The data show that, in altricial birds, fledging period is often about the same as incubation period, sometimes longer, seldom shorter, and rarely more than slightly so. In most precocial birds, fledging period is sometimes the same as incubation period, almost never shorter, and often longer to very much longer. Exceptions with short fledging periods are found primarily among the megapodes and other ground-nesting galliforms, but in some charadriiforms as well (Jehl, 1975; Skutch, 1976:201). Lack wrestled with the problem of incubation-fledging periods for at least twenty years and concluded that:

there is a general correlation in birds between the lengths of the incubation and fledging periods, the reason for which is not clear, but I have tentatively suggested that perhaps the easiest way to evolve a different growth rate in the nestlings is to change it throughout the growth period, including that of the embryo in the egg; I am not happy about this, but can think of no better explanation... (1968:174-175).

In other words, there may be advantages in having a genetically determined slow rate of post-hatching development, and this usually cannot be uncoupled from a slow prehatching rate, that is, a long incubation period. There are only two obvious general advantages to a long post-hatching development period: (1) to allow for the maturation of complex systems (such as the flight apparatus of the long-winged procellariiforms) essential for survival of a particular adaptive type; and (2) to have a growth rate slow enough that the ability of the parent birds to provide food is not inadequate for the metabolic needs of the young. Lack (1948, 1968) emphasized the latter situation. In either case, the inference is that relatively long incubation periods exist as a consequence of selection for a long fledging period, and the advantages of the latter must be sought to account for the former.

The extension of this inference to the EP suggests that its long incubation period, which involves great risks and has no obvious advantages, must be a corollay of a long fledging period which does have some advantages. It is difficult to see any advantage of a long fledging period to a young bird thereby confined to an island and exposed to aerial predators. If my estimation of 35 days as the approximate fledging period is correct, then this period is not prolonged but is only slightly beyond the relative minimum for most precocial birds, which is about equal to the incubation period. This invites re-examination of the question of whether there may be some advantage to a long incubation period as such, considered independently of fledging period.

One potential advantage of a long incubation period is that it allows time for more advanced development of the chick before hatching. Vleck et al. (1979) provide new data on oxygen consumption during pre-hatching development and summarize previous findings. In brief, the metabolic rate of the embryo of altricial species increases exponentially to the time of hatching, with growth in embryonic mass continuing throughout the incubation period. In precocial species, the metabolic rate levels off several days before hatching, and it approaches a plateau stage during that interval although there is some fluctuation. Presumably, this plateau indicates that the phase of rapid growth in embryonic mass has been succeeded by a period of developmental maturation that results in the precocial condition by the time of hatching. The greater the degree of maturation of such systems as sense organs and neuromuscular complexes, the greater the behavioral capabilities of the hatchling.

This is not to say that a prolonged incubation period is essential to or necessarily correlates with the production of precocial chicks. In many shorebirds, especially those that breed in the arctic where the nesting season is short, selection has favored relatively large eggs and apparently minimal incubation periods compatible with a high degree of pre-hatching development. Most of these species avoid predation through inconspicuous nest sites and highly cryptic patterns of adults, eggs, and chicks. In contrast, the EP produces relatively small eggs with a long incubation period. Its nesting sites are so exposed and the adults so conspicuous that only precocial chicks that on the day of hatching can run effectively, get to water, and respond appropriately to parental actions would have much chance of survival. The EP has achieved the essential precocial condition, but through adaptations in directions opposite to those shown by many charadriiform species.

As the EP is the only riverine courser it is presumably derived from dry-habitat ancestors comparable to the other African species listed on p. 55. Most of these also have relatively small eggs, and the EP's egg size probably reflects in part the courser ancestry. The clearest advantage to having a small egg is that less energy and body resources are required to produce it. As shown on p. 55, the EP puts only about one-half as much of such resources into its clutch of eggs as do plovers of similar adult body weight and clutch size. The vigorous activity of both sexes of the EP for a long period during establishment and defense of a nesting territory may constitute an energy drain so great as to counter any trend toward the evolution of larger eggs. Given the relatively small egg of the EP, the long incubation period may allow for more pre-hatching maturation and the emergence of a more precocial chick than would otherwise be the case. A prolongation of the incubation period is possible only if, among other thngs, the eggs are well concealed and the amount of (irreplaceable) water lost is not too great. Covering with sand provides maximum concealment, and egg-wetting and the consequent low rate of water loss would permit the evolution of a longer incubation period without great risk of excessive dehydration. The yolk supply would have to be adequate to provide enough energy, and in most bird species there is enough yolk that some is retained in the gut of the chick and metabolized after hatching. The EP chick may be able to afford to use more of its yolk stores for pre-hatching development because food is brought by the parents on the day of hatching and to some extent on subsequent days, and because it is also aided in feeding itself by parental guidance.

Chicks of other species of coursers are also fed by their parents, but no other courser species is known to have an incubation period as long as that of the EP. The available data indicate that the young of other coursers are slightly less precocial at hatching (Maclean, pers. comm.). Maclean's study (1967) of the Double-banded Courser, *Rhinoptilus africanus,* gives the incubation period as at least 25 but less than 28 days, and he describes the newly-hatched chick as

> ... almost naked and very weak, but its eyes are open and bright... As the down dries the chick appears less naked... The chick leaves the nest within 24 hours, but does not move more than a few yards from the nest for the first 3 or 4 days after hatching. Both parents feed it at frequent intervals, bringing small insects in the bill... It is probably able to feed itself within a week, but the parents continue to feed it occasionally until it is almost ready to fly when about six weeks old. (Maclean, 1967:563).

From this description I would estimate that the degree of development of the EP at hatching is comparable to that of *R. africanus* at the post-hatching age of about four days; the EP also seems to have a shorter fledging period by about one week. The total time of development in the two species from egg-laying to fledging seems approximately equal, but the EP appears in comparison to have a lengthened incubation period and a correspondingly shortened fledging period.

Chicks of the EP are also reported to be able to swim and dive. Serle (1939) stated without specific examples that the young can "swim well." Fry (1966) observed a recently-hatched EP chick diving and swimming under water using its downy wings. I never saw an EP chick enter water deep enough to require swimming, but Fry's account leaves no doubt that the chicks do this on occasion—further evidence of precocity and adaptation to the fluviatile habitat. Ability to swim would enable chicks to cross some channels to other islands in the pre-fledging period and would certainly be advantageous. In most parts of the swift-flowing Baro River, however, there would be a great risk of being swept away and drowned or eaten by the abundant predatory fish. Because of this risk I did not attempt to force chicks into the water to test their ability to swim and dive.

In summary, the EP chick shows a high degree of precocity even though it hatches from an egg that is unusually small in relation to the body size of the adult. I suggest that the unusually long incubation period of the EP egg may be adaptive in that it allows time for the maturation of systems necessary for such precocity at the time of hatching.

PHYLOGENY

I have based the following attempt to reconstruct the phylogeny of the EP on the data presented in this study and on the evidence that the EP is a member of the Subfamily Cursoriinae. [Yudin (1961) suggested on the basis of the jaw mechanism that *Pluvianus* may not be a member of the Charadriiformes. This suggestion is totally unsupported by the evidence from external morphology, behavior, and ecology.] I will attempt to show how the behavior of the EP is integrated with the ecological conditions of its nesting habitat in ways that contribute to reproductive success.

I propose that the EP is derived from ancestral stock similar to that which gave rise to the present-day coursers. Other than the EP, these are all inhabitants of hot arid habitats and are essentially nondimorphic, cryptically-colored ground nesters. The EP represents a different adaptive type that has colonized a habitat not occupied by other coursers nor used for nesting by most other African charadriiforms—the transient river sandbars which emerge during the dry season. These provide a loose, sandy substrate similar to that used for nesting by other coursers and also increasing foraging opportunities as the water level continues to fall. The selection of insular sandbars (determined by foraging entirely around them) would provide protection from terrestrial predators, but the use of such sandbars introduces new problems including exposure to full sun and, potentially, limitation of the chicks to a restricted area until they are able to fly. Colonization of this habitat for nesting would necessitate adaptations to cope with (1) intense solar heat; (2) concealment of the nest; (3) protection of available food resources from competitors; (4) protection from predators (primarily aerial) from the time of egg-laying to fledging of the young. If these difficulties could be overcome, a niche otherwise unoccupied by coursers could be filled. In retrospect, it appears that the EP has successfully adapted as required and thrives along tropical African rivers where man has not drastically altered primordial conditions.

It is impossible to present multiple, branching, phylogenetic events in a linear sequence, but this is the obligatory form of narrative writing and it must be used to approximate the postulated sequences. I suggest the following events:

Nesting on open sandbars exposed to full sun requires adaptations in parallel. Eggs (and later chicks) must be concealed from predators, and overheating must be avoided. Covering the eggs with sand meets the first requirement and goes part way toward meeting the second. Concealing the eggs by covering with sand is a well-developed behavior pattern in some charadriiforms, including some other coursers. Wetting of the eggs with water carried in the ventral feathers is also widespread among charadriiforms. By combining these two practices, the EP established a new adaptive pattern. Not only was concealment achieved, but the eggs could be left for longer periods during threats of danger as eggs buried in wet sand would not heat up as fast as those openly exposed to full sun or covered only with dry sand. Because even shaded air temperatures at ground level on the sandbars may reach as high as 46°C, shading alone of unburied, unwetted eggs would be insufficient to keep egg temperatures below lethal levels. Burying in dry sand would not provide adequate protection as temperatures at buried-egg depth in unshaded dry sand reach levels that would be lethal for eggs (figs. 2-4). Simple wetting of exposed eggs would not be adequate either as water would quickly evaporate from the egg surfaces and would provide no further cooling.

The combined concealment and wetting of the eggs makes it possible for the adult EPs to leave the nest for many minutes when danger threatens, even during the hottest part of the day. With egg-covering and wetting as established patterns, conspicuousness of adults would not be selected against if it otherwise provided significant advantages such as in the defense of territory. Egg-burial also provides both adults with several hours of free time for foraging in the early morning and late afternoon when, with little or no parental attendance, egg temperature remains within the range of normal incubation temperature.

Even though the eggs are buried and wetted they will reach lethally high internal temperatures if left unattended too long. This risk probably requires that both parents take equal roles in nest care; otherwise, more than a few minutes' absence at an unfavorable time by the mate that would usually attend the nest could result in heat death of the embryos. Defense of the resources within the nesting territory also seems to require equal participation of both sexes, which would further the selection of a conspicuous monomorphic plumage pattern.

The use of a sandbar island — even a small one — as a breeding territory, and its frequent, active defense requires the almost continuous presence of a territorial bird. This in turn requires that whichever bird is present finds adequate food on that island or on closely adjacent areas. This appears possible for the EP because of its highly diverse feeding methods (surface-picking, probing, digging, jump-scratching, stone-turning, fly-catching) that allow an unusually full exploitation of the available arthropod resources. These diverse feeding methods are also valuable in making food available to young birds not fully able to find their own. The close association of parents and young for several weeks after hatching must aid the young birds in developing skill in locating food. The timing of nesting is also advantageous in this respect, as the overall trend in the dry season (despite short-term reversals) is for water level in the rivers to decline, thus exposing new foraging areas at the time that the young birds must become more independent.

The fact that the EP nests only along rivers that provide emergent sandbars and not around lakeshores with similar sandy substrates shows that the species has multiple special requirements and is adapted to a particular type of fluviatile environment. The set of necessary environmental conditions does not appear to be unusual or highly restricted geographically, and the limitation of the EP's range to only a portion (albeit a large one) of the African continent indicates that the species probably differentiated within that area.

The association of the EP with *Homo sapiens* in Africa dates back many thousands of years and the bird appears to have adapted adequately to the presence of mankind in the absence of modern technology. The impact of modern man on the nature of riverine habitats, however, has generally been in the direction of changes unfavorable to the EP. Modern man's objectives are usually to reduce great seasonal fluctuations of water level, to keep rivers navigable for vessels larger than shallow-draft dugouts, and in general to regularize conditions. Given these trends, I think it unlikely that the EP will expand its range beyond the present limits, but it should maintain its numbers in those regions in which relatively natural conditions along rivers remain unchanged.

REFERENCES

Anderson, J. 1898. Zoology of Egypt: vol. 1. Reptilia and Batrachia. London, B. Quaritch. Reprinted 1965, Codicote, Herts., Wheldon & Wesley.
Ar, A., C. V. Paganelli, R. B. Reeves, D. G. Greene, and H. Rahn. 1974. The avian egg: water vapor conductance, shell thickness, and functional pore area. Condor 76:153-158.
Archer, G. F., and E. M. Godman. 1937. The birds of British Somaliland and the Gulf of Aden; their life histories, breeding habits, and eggs, vol. 2. London, Gurney and Jackson, 290-626 p.
Bellow, S. 1959. Henderson, the rain king; a novel. New York, Viking Press, 341 p.
Brehm, A. E. 1854. Zur Fortpflanzungsgeschichte einiger Vögel Nord-Ost-Afrika's. J. f. Ornith. 1, Extra-Heft: 93-105.
———. 1879. Thierleben, 2d ed., Vögel, vol. 6, Leipzig, Bibliographisches Institut, 671 p.
Butler, A. L. 1905. A contribution to the ornithology of the Egyptian Soudan. Ibis, series 8, 5:301-401.
———. 1931. The chicks of the Egyptian Plover. Ibis, series 13, 1:345-347.
Cade, T. J. and G. L. Maclean. 1967. Transport of water by adult sandgrouse to their young. Condor 69:323-343.
Conway, W. G., and J. Bell. 1968. Observations on the behavior of Kittlitz's Sandplovers at the New York Zoological Park. Living Bird 7th annual: 57-70.
Cott, H. B. 1962. Scientific results of an inquiry into the ecology and economic status of the Nile Crocodile (*Crocodilus niloticus*) in Uganda and Northern Rhodesia. Trans. Zool. Soc. London, 29, part 4, 211-356.
Drent, R. 1970. Functional aspects of incubation in the Herring Gull (*Larus argentatus* Pont.). Behaviour, suppl. 17, 132 p.
Flieg, G. M. 1973. Breeding biology and behaviour of the South African Hemipode in captivity. Avicultural Magazine 79:55-59.
Flower, S. S. 1908. The Egyptian Plover. *Pluvianus aegyptius*. Its name, distribution, known and reputed habits. Avicultural Magazine, new series, 6:139-144.
Frith, H. J. 1962. The Mallee Fowl. Sydney, Angus & Robertson, 136 p.
Fry, C. H. 1966. Escape-diving in Egyptian-plover chick and black crake. Bull. Nigerian Orn. Soc. 3:96.
Gatter, W. 1971. Wassertransport beim Flussregenpfeifer (*Charadrius dubius*). Vögelwelt 92:100-103.
George Kainady, P. V., and K. Y. Al-Dabbagh. 1976. Some observations on the behaviour of incubating *Charadrius alexandrinus* on hot summer days. Bulletin Barash Nat. Hist. Mus., 3:121-137.
Gould, J. 1969. Birds of Asia; illustrations from the lithographs of John Gould; text by A. Rutgers. London, Methuen & Co., 321 p.
Graul, W. D. 1973. Adaptive aspects of the Mountain Plover social system. Living Bird 12th annual: 69-94.
Guggisberg, C. A. W. 1972. Crocodiles: their natural history, folklore and conservation. Harrisburg, Pa., Stackpole Books, 195 p.
Hall, K. R. L. 1958. Observations on the nesting sites and nesting behaviour of the Kittlitz's Sandplover *Charadrius pecuarius*. Ostrich 29:113-125.
———. 1959. Nest records and additional behaviour notes for Kittlitz's Sandplover *Charadrius pecuarius* in the S.W. Cape Province. Ostrich 30:33-38.
———. 1960. Egg covering by the White-fronted Sandplover *Charadrius marginatus*. Ibis 102:545-553.
Heinroth, O. 1922. Die Beziehungen zwischen Vogelgewicht, Eigewicht, Gelegegewicht und Brutdauer. J. f. Ornith. 70:175-285.
Hoesch, W. 1960. Zum Brutverhalten des Laufhühnchens *Turnix sylvatica lepurana*. J. f. Ornith. 101:265-275.
Hoyt, D. F. 1979. Practical methods of estimating volume and fresh weight of bird eggs. Auk 96:73-77.
Hutson, H. P. W., and D. A. Bannerman. 1931. The birds of northern Nigeria. Part II. Phasianidae-Laridae. Ibis, series 13, 1:18-43.
Jehl, J. R., Jr. 1975. *Pluvianellus socialis*: biology, ecology, and relationships of an enigmatic Patagonian shorebird. Trans. San Diego Soc. Nat. Hist. 18:29-73.
Jourdain, F. C. R., and R. Shuel. 1935. Notes on a collection of eggs and breeding-habits of birds near Lokoja, Nigeria. Ibis, series 13, 5:623-663.
Kazantzakis, N. 1958. The odyssey: a modern sequel. Transl. by K. Friar. New York, Simon & Schuster, 824 p.
Kemp, A. C. and G. L. Maclean. 1973. Nesting of the Three-banded Courser. Ostrich 44:82-83.

Kendeigh, S. C. 1952. Parental care and its evolution in birds. Illinois Biol. Monogr., vol. 22, Urbana, Ill., University of Illinois Press, 356 p.

Knowlton, F. H. 1909. Birds of the world, a popular account. New York, Holt, 873 p.

Koenig, A. 1926. Ein weiterer Teilbeitrag zur Avifauna Aegyptiaca... der Wat-oder Sumpfvögel (*Grallatores*). J. f. Ornith. 74, Sonderheft, 311 p.

Lack, D. 1948. The significance of clutch-size. Part III—some interspecific comparisons, Ibis 90:25-45.

———. 1967. Interrelationships in breeding adaptations as shown by marine birds. Proc. 14th Int. Ornith. Congr.: 3-42.

———. 1968. Ecological adaptations for breeding in birds. London, Methuen & Co., 409 p.

Mackworth-Praed, C. W., and C. H. B. Grant. 1952. Birds of eastern and north eastern Africa, series I, vol. 1, London, Longmans, Green and Co., 846 p.

———. 1970. Birds of west central and western Africa, series 3, vol. 1, London, Longman, 671 p.

Maclean, G. L. 1967. The breeding biology and behaviour of the Double-banded Courser *Rhinoptilus africanus* (Temminck). Ibis 109:556-569.

———. 1974. Egg-covering in the Charadrii. Ostrich 45:167-174.

———. 1975. Belly-soaking in the Charadriformes. J. Bombay Nat. Hist. Soc. 72:74-82.

Meinertzhagen, R. 1959. Pirates and predators. Edinburgh and London, Oliver & Boyd, 230 p.

Newton, A. 1893-1896. A dictionary of birds. London, A. and C. Black, 1088 p.

Nice, M. M. 1954a. Problems of incubation periods in North American birds. Condor 56:173-197.

———. 1954b. Incubation periods throughout the ages. Centaurus 3:311-359.

———. 1962. Development of behavior in precocial birds. Trans. Linn. Soc. New York, 8, 211 p.

Ogilvie-Grant, W. R. and R. McD. Hawker. 1902. On a collection of birds made on the White Nile between Khartum and Fashoda. Ibis, series 8, 2:393-470.

Paganelli, C. V., A. Olszowka, and A. Ar. 1974. The avian egg: surface area, volume and density. Condor 76:319-325.

Percival, W. G. 1906. Habits of young Egyptian Plovers. Avicultural Magazine, series 2, 4:293.

Perrins, C. 1976. Birds: their life, their ways, their world. New York, Abrams, 160 p.

Rahn, H., R. A. Ackerman and C. V. Paganelli. 1977. Humidity in the avian nest and egg water loss during incubation. Physiol. Zool. 50:269-283.

Rahn, H. and A. Ar. 1974. The avian egg: incubation time and water loss. Condor 76:147-152.

Rahn, H., C. V. Paganelli, and A. Ar. 1975. Relation of avian egg weight to body weight. Auk 92:750-765.

Rahn, H., C. V. Paganelli, I. C. T. Nisbet, and G. C. Whittow. 1976. Regulation of incubation water loss in eggs of seven species of terns. Physiol. Zool. 49:245-259.

Rautenberg, W., R. Necker and B. May. 1972. Thermoregulatory responses of the pigeon to changes of the brain and the spinal cord temperatures. Pflügers Arch. 338:31-42.

Rey, E. 1899. Die Eier der Vögel Mitteleuropas, vol. 1, Gera-Untermhaus, Köhler.

Roberts, M. G. 1977. Belly-soaking in the Whitefronted Plover. Ostrich 48:111-112.

Schönwetter, M. 1960. Handbuch der Oölogie, vol. 1. Berlin, Akademie Verlag.

Seebohm, H. 1888. The geographical distribution of the family Charadriidae, or the plovers, sandpipers, snipes and their allies. London, Sotheran, 524 p.

Serle, W. 1939. Field observations on some northern Nigerian birds. Ibis, series 14, 3:654-699.

Skutch, A. F. 1957. The incubation patterns of birds. Ibis 99:69-93.

———. 1976. Parent birds and their young. Austin, University of Texas Press, 503 p.

Stresemann, E. 1927-1934. Sauropsida: Aves. *In* Kukenthal and Krumbach, eds., Handb. der Zoologie, vol. 7, part 2, Berlin and Leipzig, de Gruyter & Co., 899 p.

Vleck, C. M., D. F. Hoyt, and D. Vleck. 1979. Metabolism of avian embryos: patterns in altricial and precocial species. Physiol. Zool. 52:363-377.

von Heuglin, M. T. 1873. Ornithologie Nordost-Afrika's, der Nilguellen- und Kusten-Gebiete des Rothen Meeres und des nordlichen Somal-Landes, vol. 2. Cassel, Fischer.

Walsberg, G. E., G. S. Campbell, and J. R. King. 1978. Animal coat color and radiative heat gain: a reevaluation. J. Comp. Physiol. 126:211-222.

Yudin, K. A. 1961. (On the mechanism of the jaw in the Charadriiformes, Procellariiformes, and some other birds.) Trudy. Zool. Inst. Leningrad 29:257-302.

PLATES

PLATE 1
Posture typical of intraspecific threat display (p. 20).

PLATE 2
Interspecific threat display, wing-waving phase; one secondary feather of bird's right wing is displaced.

PLATE 3
Looking-up (p. 19) by brooding adult during hot mid-day period; note ruffling of body feathers and elevation of elongate black mid-dorsal feathers (p. 11).

PLATE 4
Attack on Black Kite, *Milvus migrans;* one bird has attracted kite's attention in front while mate harasses kite from behind.

PLATE 5
Alert posture of adult with newly-hatched chicks; note wet ventral feathers.

PLATE 6
Interspecific threat display directed toward Striped Thick-knee, *Burhinus senegalensis*.

PLATE 7
Pair at preliminary nest-scrapes; bird in background is in V-tilt posture (p. 24).

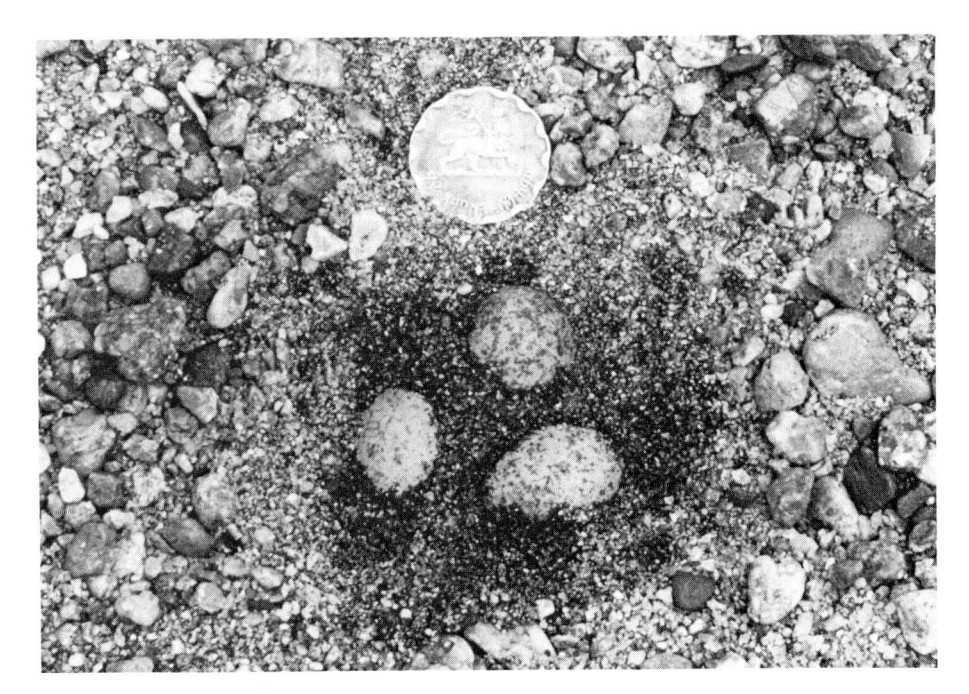

PLATE 8
A. Clutch of eggs uncovered for photographing; diameter of coin = 23 mm.
B. Clutch of eggs partly uncovered for photographing; dark area marks extent of wet sand.

PLATE 9
A. First stage of covering eggs or chicks with sand; note open bill.
B. Using bill only, adult throws sand over two chicks; eggs are covered in identical manner.

PLATE 10
Final stage of soaking (p. 31), showing bill-dip with slightly open bill; note blurring of posterior region, indicating continuing rocking movement.

PLATE 11
Adult with soaked ventral feathers settling on newly-hatched chicks, as is also done with eggs in nest.

PLATE 12
Chick hatching from egg 1b (table 1); chick from egg 1a had left nest; remaining egg 1c was hatched the next morning; extent of uncovering is as found after attending parent was flushed.

PLATE 13
Recently-hatched chick at river's edge for drinking and bathing.

PLATE 14
A. Two recently-hatched chicks (from eggs 1a-b, table 1) covered with sand by adult, slightly exposed for photographing.
B. The two chicks more fully exposed.

PLATE 14
C. The two chicks fully exposed but remaining immobile; diameter of coin = 23 mm.

PLATE 15
A. Juvenile, age about three weeks, largely covered with sand by adult at site where sand was sparse; the bird's head points to the lower left.
B. The juvenile after excavation from sand; it remained immobile until extensively handled.
(Enlarged from 16 mm cine film)

Forsyth Library
F.H.S.U.

ISBN 0-520-03